STOP OVERTHINKING

Get Rid of the Mental Habits that Cause you to Over-Analyze and Worry About Things that don't Need to be Worried About
(2022 Guide for Beginners)

Elaine Mack

TABLE OF CONTENTS

INTRODUCTION

There are two types of overthinking syndrome:

1. Speculating about the future

2. Reflecting on the past

The two are not the same as issue solving since problem-solving entails discovering or imagining the optimal answer. It takes into consideration ruminating on the subject while overthinking.

Overthinking, on the other hand, is not synonymous with self-reflection.

A good self-reflection is all about learning something about yourself and gaining a fresh perspective on any scenario. Self-reflection is determined, determined, and resolute.

Overthinking is defined as lingering on how startling and dreadful you feel and pondering about things over which you have no complete control.

This mental state will not assist the person in developing a fresh idea or insight. Rather, damage your day-to-day existence.

The difference between overthinking, self-reflection, and issue resolution is not just due to the amount of time spent in deep contemplation. It is not about the amount of time you spend developing and devising unique solutions. It is also not about how much time you spend learning if your behavior is effective or not. However, the time you spent overthinking things was not beneficial to your life. It makes no difference if it is 10 minutes, ten days, ten weeks, or ten years.

What Happens If I Excessively Worry?

Worrying is the state of being upset or too concerned about an issue or situation. When you worry excessively, your body and mind go into overdrive because you are constantly focused on what can happen.

You may suffer tension, anxiety, or even panic if you spend too much time worrying. This usually happens throughout the day. Many persons who have this illness report feeling false panics, anxiety, or imminent doom, which further adds to their fears. Worriers or overthinkers may regard everybody and everything as a potential danger if they are too receptive and sensitive to what others say, including their environment.

Too much worry may have an impact on a person's day-to-day existence. This might interfere with his or her nutrition, sleep, and relationships with family and friends. Too much worry may also have an impact on one's living choices and performance at work. Many individuals who overthink are so stressed out that they seek relief in unhealthy lifestyle habits such as cigarette smoking, overeating, drug use, and excessive drinking.

Too many worrying results in an inability to regulate upsetting, recurring pictures and thoughts. The procedure might be somewhat annoying or highly engrossing. Obsessive pictures and ideas are embedded in a complex network of sensations, emotions, and, in most cases, behavioral patterns. According to brain imaging studies, overthinking is connected to an undiscovered neurological disorder that forces the mind into recurrent loops. While many individuals are overthinking for the first time, others may have experienced recurring episodes, with the exact and specific substance shifting over time. Overthinking, experts say, is like a hamster wheel: when one rodent gets off, another takes its place, and the wheel continues to spin.

Overthinking is adaptive when it is used to healthy goals and real-world problems with achievable solutions. On the other hand, for a large number of individuals, this method no longer works. We're here to talk about the negative consequences of overthinking: preoccupation, rumination, and concern.

Worry

Worry is defined as an anxious preoccupation with occurrences that are expected or anticipated. Healthy concern forewarns the person about potential problems and supports problem solutions. If an issue is being solved, the anxiety or worry will gradually fade away.

Acceptance is acquired after it is determined that there is no definite or obvious answer and that direct change over the unneeded problem is not possible.

On the other side, the adaptive process fails the majority of the time. Our minds get engrossed in a never-ending process of "figuring it out." We were overcome by sights and ideas of disastrous outcomes that may never occur. Concerns or fears are fueled by difficulties that lack a clear and specific answer. As a result, rather than managing and accepting these truths, they are seen as evidence of the futility of attempting to figure things out.

Rumination

You spend more time reflecting on incidents that have transpired in the past. It's a fixation on confessed flaws, slights, and losses; acts that weren't done, and opportunities that were never taken.

Envy, rage, remorse, and guilt are all sentiments associated with preoccupied rumination. Most of the time, rumination is associated with complaints, grudges, and judgments directed at others or both self and others. The overpowering idea that if only things had been different, existing and future unhappiness and melancholy might have been averted.

The Damage Has Already Been Done

Overthinking has the potential to prolong and exacerbate an uncomfortable emotional state. This syndrome may also promote detrimental behavioral patterns and communication. Concern, problem, or anxiety may amplify unpleasant and restless sensations, which means you fear yourself, resulting in even more issues. This might cause anxiety to continue for hours, days, weeks, months, or even years. At the moment, this leads to terror attacks and an emotional spike of humiliation, guilt, and rage.

Furthermore, ruminating exacerbates sentiments of rage, despair, and melancholy. When this sensation is taken for granted, it may lead to despair and withdrawal. It may also lead to destructive outbursts of fury and hostility. Overthinking associated with OCD may be debilitating or distracting. And compulsive harmful practices may slowly erode your health and lifestyle. Overall, it knocks a person off his or her game.

Obsessive thinking is quite common. On the other side, there is assistance available for this kind of problem. Many people suffer from overthinking everything that is beyond their control.

I. Signs You Have an Overthinking Mind

If you have a problem stemming from your emotions and thoughts and are always stressed, we have a variety of solutions below to help you stop overthinking. But first, we'd want to show you some of the most prevalent signs that you're trapped in an overthinking mind.

Here are several indicators:

Consistent Insomnia

Insomnia may hit you because you are unable to turn off your brain, and your ideas gradually immobilize you. Your mind races, and you find it difficult to sleep. Worries remain in your head, and you can't get out of this situation.

If you have this symptom, it is best to conduct some soothing activities before going to bed, such as yoga, writing, reading, meditating, and chatting to someone. Do something to distract yourself from negative thoughts.

You live in terror. Nolen-Hoeksema observed that fear motivates people to consume alcohol, smoke, and take drugs to block out their terrible thoughts.

If you have this symptom, you should attempt meditation or other approaches that promote awareness. Allow ten to twenty minutes every day to vent your frustrations, whether by conversing with friends or singing. You can go about your day without worrying if you do it this way.

You overthink things. The major problem with overthinkers is that they feel compelled to manage everything. They need to alter the future, but they can't since they can't predict it, which causes them worry and grief. Overthinkers don't want to cope with anything they can't manage. They are so afraid of the situation that they ponder the options rather than acting to fix the problem.

Overthinking, according to research done at UC Santa Barbara, leads to poor judgment and decision making.

Fear of Failure

Overthinkers also have a never-ending ambition for perfection in whatever they undertake. They are incapable of accepting failure. They go to great lengths in their ruling to avoid it. Surprisingly, this generally consists of doing nothing. Remember that fear may immobilize an overthinker. As a result, rather than risking failing, they did not place themselves in a position to fail.

Constantly second-guessing

Overthinkers constantly scrutinize and re-analyze every issue because they strive for perfection. They are terrified of making the incorrect decision. As a result, individuals spend their time making decisions since they lack confidence in their options. Overthinkers are also disconnected from their instincts. As a result, each decision is made by their brain, which is not a good thing. If your mind is bogged down and murky, and you are unable to make a decent decision, you are most likely an overthinker.

You may overcome this issue by learning how to trust your instincts. If you made a bad judgment, don't worry; the most important thing is that you learned from your error.

Constant Migraines

If you get recurring headaches, you may be overanalyzing things. A headache indicates that your mind and body need to relax. If you pay attention to your thoughts, you may notice that you think about the same things again and over.

Muscles and joints that are stiff

Overthinking has an impact on your muscles, joints, and other bodily components. If your body is harmed, it will affect your mental state as well. Unless the root cause is treated, you will be plagued by sadness and agony indefinitely. Overthinking begins in our brain, but it affects our physical and emotional well-being, leaving us lethargic and fatigued.

In general, you should focus on activities that you love and that drives you to keep active. You may join an exercise program and meet positive individuals. You may also consume healthful meals, cultivate mindfulness, and, perhaps most importantly, learn to accept reality. You must also understand how to have a healthy relationship with yourself. Consider your ideas to be a tool for learning new things in life, rather than a problem that hinders your growth.

II. Can Obsessive Thinking Lead to Stress?

Pressures and stress are often generated from the wants and fears we face daily. Heavy traffic, lengthy lineups at department stores, nonstop ringing of cellphones, deadlines that must be reached, harsh supervisors, picky and difficult-to-understand coworkers, and serious medical issues. These are some of the factors that might contribute to stress.

When stress and anxieties become extreme, there is a probability that the stress response may be triggered.

When it comes to stress reaction, there are two things to keep in mind at all times. The first is awareness of the challenge, and the second is the instinctive physiological response, commonly known as the "fight or flight" reflex, which results in a surge of adrenaline.

Our bodies are put on high alert as a result of this. Physiological instinctive reaction shielded our forefathers from dangers such as wild animals that might easily make a meal of them. Even though we do not commonly meet wild creatures at this stage, damages and hazards still exist. These threats might take the shape of colicky children, demanding coworkers, or a conflict with family members.

III. Can Overthinking Cause Physical Illness?

Obsessive thinking and stress may cause a variety of health problems. The issue arises when an innate physiological reaction drives our sympathetic nervous system to produce cortisol, a form of stress hormone. Cortisol can raise blood sugar and blood fat levels, which our bodies may use as fuel.

Cortisol may also cause bodily reactions that take into consideration the following:

Mouth Dryness

Dizziness

Swallowing Difficulties

Palpitation (rapid heartbeat)

Stress or exhaustion

Headaches

Focus lapse

unable to focus

Muscle spasms and tension

Irritability

Nervous vitality

Nausea

Shortness of breath and rapid breathing

Twitching

Trembling

Sweating

If there is too much fuel in our blood for physical activity, the intense anxiety and outburst of cortisol might have long-term bodily consequences. These findings take into consideration the following factors:

Suppression of the immune system

You have muscular tension.

Digestive problems

Early coronary artery disease

Immediate memory loss

The heart attack

Obsessive thinking and persistent stress, if ignored and mistreated, may lead to despair and suffering, as well as aggravate suicide thoughts.

Even though these consequences are caused by stress, stress is just the catalyst. It makes no difference whether you get ill or have bad health since it is all dependent on how you manage your stress. Our immune system, blood vessels, and heart all respond to stress in different ways.

Stress reactions also affect how certain glands in our bodies produce hormones. These hormones serve an important role in regulating several bodily activities, including nerve impulses and brain function.

These systems are interconnected. They are profoundly influenced by our emotional and mental responses to the illness. It is not the stress and worry that causes us to get unwell. Instead, it is the influence of emotions such as excessive thinking and concern on these many interacting systems that may cause physical illness. However, there are other things you can do, including adjustments in your lifestyle, to alter the way you react and respond.

CHAPTER 1:

VARIOUS CAUSES OF OVERTHINKING

Overthinking various life conditions and other trivial matters is a widespread problem these days. It doesn't mean that educating yourself or thinking about your problems is bad, but if you have a proclivity to twist things around in your mind until you see it from every angle and possibility, you are an over-thinker. For some people, ruminating about various topics and events is a natural part of life. It generally leads people to explore solutions to their problems and prepares them to face life's difficulties and conquer obstacles.

There are several advantages and disadvantages to being an over-thinker. Do you want to discover why those bothersome thoughts regarding various situations drive you to overthink? Continue reading to uncover several undeniable reasons why you overthink your problems.

1. You are unable to relax.

It commonly happens that you can't get your mind off the problem you can't stop thinking about. Many sensitive people live in constant stress because they don't know how to unwind and replace the cycle of negative thoughts with good ones.

Yoga is the most effective way to distract yourself from overthinking. Yoga is an excellent tool for quieting your rich creative mind and relieving your stress over the issue. Simply sit and visualize a happy place that makes you feel certain, free, and fulfilled.

2. A persistent worrisome

3. Lack of certainty

One of the primary causes of overthinking is a lack of certainty. When you procrastinate about doing things, you allow vulnerability and anxiety to into your mind. No one can predict where your decisions will take you, which is why you should step out on a limb without torturing yourself. When you start making decisions, you will be able to increase your certainty. When you are assured and firm, you will conquer any difficulties without even putting in a reasonable effort.

4. Overthinking is just a habit.

Overthinking your problems and constantly researching your actions may quickly turn into an unfavorable habit. This proclivity often prevents you from living a happy life. It is difficult to break this mind-desensitizing habit, but you should always try to catch yourself overthinking and alter these bothersome thoughts. When you see your mind beginning to provide a dramatization, you should immerse yourself in some interesting and engaging activity. It will assist you in overcoming overthinking. Thinking is an unavoidable part of your life that helps you accomplish goals and avoid annoyances; nevertheless, you need to understand the distinction between thinking and overthinking. Overthinking matters may have a detrimental impact on your well-being.

5. Overthinking is a kind of security

Some people acknowledge that overthinking may be a kind of protection against difficulties. Overthinking is a trap that is suffocating your progress. There is a greater benefit to action than passivity since interactions help you grow and become more grounded. Overthinking increases both your insurance and your chances of missing an opportunity since your mind is always debating the situation and scrabbling for another solution.

6. You must be spotless.

You should be aware that the costs of being a stickler are substantial. Many people who struggle with compulsive behavior spend their lives on edge all the time.

Hairsplitting leads to overthinking since sticklers are always striving to be better. They may also wake up in the middle of the night worrying about what has to be done. Such a style of living may wreak havoc on your psychological and physical well-being. You should understand that no one is perfect, and it is better to get rid of the tendency to overthink everything.

7. Reconsidering yourself

It is better to make decisions more quickly and efficiently. Simply get rid of the propensity to second-guess oneself.

Re-thinking causes you to go over the situation in your head over and again because you suspect you haven't done things correctly. As a result, you are either perpetually dissatisfied or certain that you have made the perfect option. Attempt to become more confident in yourself and your abilities. It will allow you to be less focused on your easygoing choices during the day.

CHAPTER 2:

THE CONNECTION BETWEEN OVERTHINKING AND ANXIETY, STRESS, AND PESSIMISTIC THINKING

It's amazing to discover that our ideas shape what occurs to us.

From a psychological standpoint, this suggests that we can influence what occurs to us by learning how to regulate our thoughts. This is an effective strategy. The fact that you have control over what occurs to you is something that most people are not aware of.

The truth is that you become what you think about. If you look carefully, you will see that everything that occurs to you, good or bad, starts from your ideas.

Your mental health and well-being are influenced by what you think about. Your ideas are the source of whatever emotional state you may be feeling.

This frequently has an impact on your health. If your thoughts are consumed with terrible situations, you will most likely feel sad all of the time. If you are continuously thinking about the exciting things you do with your friends, you will draw the same energy into your life.

This will give you a better understanding of why your thoughts might be the source of your diminishing productivity at work, lack of sleep, and deteriorating social interactions.

The Universal Law of Attraction

If you are worried about the course of your life, the law of attraction may be a great tool to help you get back on track.

On the surface, it seems that this is a law that assists you in attracting things around you. As the name implies, this is a strong rule that states that you attract what you concentrate on. [9]

Whether you believe it or not, this rule is constantly shaping your life. What most people don't realize is that they are continuously molding their life, whether consciously or unconsciously. What you thought about

19

years ago has resulted in the life you live now. You may not receive precisely what you desired, but you will be better off than if you think negatively.

Your future is formed by how you think and react to things right now. As a result, if you anticipate that the approaching months will be tough for you, you can be certain that they will be. On the other hand, if you believe you are going to have fun, you are more likely to enjoy life as it unfolds according to your expectations.

The law of attraction is based on a straightforward notion. What you choose to focus on attracts you. It is entirely up to you whether you choose to think negatively or positively. If you choose to concentrate on the positive aspects of life, you will attract wonderful things. You will always be full of joy and plenty; you will go through life feeling energized and ready to face whatever comes your way. On the other hand, if you choose to dwell on the bad, your life will be miserable; you will never be satisfied with the people around you. You will often feel as though you are sick of life. Your productivity at work and home will suffer as a result. You'll always be the person who sees the worst in everything. All of this is a result of your choice of focus.

Understanding how the law of attraction works can help you open the doors to success in your life. This law awakens you to the fact that we live in a world of infinite possibilities, infinite joy, and infinite abundance. Consider this: you can put your confidence in your beliefs and influence future results. Isn't it incredible? Unfortunately, few people grasp the law of attraction and how to use it successfully to change their life.

Your ideas and emotions will work together to form your perfect future. Because you can choose what you want, you should ask for the life you've always desired. Your focus and energy should be directed toward attracting what you want to attract.

How to Implement the Law of Attraction

After realizing that you are the creator of your environment, you should start thinking intentionally about how to make a better life for yourself. This should inspire you to think optimistically in this circumstance since your ideas dictate what you desire in life. This necessitates focusing your time and attention on the positive aspects of your life. It also implies that you should consciously govern your ideas and emotions since they influence what appears.

Inquire, Believe, and Receive

The law of attraction looks to be a simple procedure in which you just ask for what you desire and you will get it. The application procedure, on the other hand, needs more than merely asking and getting. If it were so easy, everyone would be enjoying joyful lives devoid of tension and anxiety. So, what is it about the law of attraction that makes it so simple yet so difficult to apply?

Every day, people send requests to the universe, whether consciously or unintentionally via their thoughts. What you think about is what you concentrate on. This is where your energy has been directed.

Using the law of attraction, you should understand how important it is to take conscious efforts to govern your thoughts and emotions.

In this regard, you must deliberately decide that you want something. This also requires you to live and act as if you already have what you are asking for.

Believe

It is critical that you truly believe that you will receive what you desire to manifest in your life. Your thoughts should reflect your confidence in knowing that you will get what you want. As a result, your mind should be clear of any uncertainties. This is the most difficult aspect of the law of attraction.

The majority of folks merely inquire. They, on the other hand, find it difficult to trust that they can receive what they desire. When people understand that what they asked for is taking longer than expected to emerge, the component of belief lessens. As a result, they focus their attention on negative thoughts. They start convincing themselves that it is impossible. It is not an easy life. Such views have no bearing on what you ask the universe for. Worst of all, negativity bias starts to take form. They unknowingly attract negativity into their lives because they simply do not believe.

Receive

The last thing you need to do is obtain what you asked for or hoped for. This may be the simplest portion since it simply asks you to position yourself in the best manner possible via your emotions to accept your gift. Consider the following scenario: you are getting a present from your loved ones. Certainly, your body language indicates that you are content. Receiving any present should elicit feelings of affection and gratitude. This is how the universe anticipates you receiving your prize.

You should spend your day being grateful and pleased for what you already have. This is the most effective technique to practice obtaining what you desire before the world offers it to you. These emotions might also be influenced by how you think.

As a result, it is advised that you live thoughtfully by increasing your self-awareness so that you can stop yourself if unpleasant ideas arise in your head.

Controlling your thoughts and emotions will be difficult at first. Nonetheless, it is worth recognizing that anything worthwhile needs patience and practice. As a result, for the law of attraction to operate for you, you must be patient. You must continue to cultivate the habit of believing. Most importantly, remember that you can create your happiness.

Stopping Negative Thoughts; Anxiety

Anxiety is produced by a variety of circumstances. It is sometimes caused by a mix of hereditary and environmental causes. The fear inside you might easily cause you to be concerned about things that have not occurred. In severe circumstances, this causes panic. Your mind may easily exaggerate your anxieties and convince you that something horrible will happen. Anxiety will keep you constantly worried about speaking the incorrect thing in front of other people in social situations. You may also come to believe that other people will not like you. Such negative ideas do nothing except keep you from being yourself. It prevents you from enjoying your life.

Anxious People's Common Thoughts

Certain stressful thoughts are noticeable in nervous persons.

Here are a few instances of some of these ideas. Identifying these ideas is beneficial since it guarantees that you find a solution to your uneasiness. The following are some examples of common ideas among nervous persons.

"I'm not very good at what I do."

Anxious people tend to concentrate on their bad qualities of themselves. In whatever situation, their brains will be preoccupied with their flaws. It will be tough for them to consider their abilities and why they were picked for a certain function at work. Anxiety, for example, will make you believe that your employer will dismiss you at any point.

"I'm sure I'll forget."

Have you ever had the feeling that you were going to forget something even before it happened? This is a symptom that you are stressed. Believing that you will forget anything merely indicates that you do not trust yourself. You're creating doubts in your mind about your ability to recall things throughout the day, tomorrow, or shortly.

"No one likes me."

In the social media environment, it's all too simple for a worried person to assume that others don't appreciate them since they don't receive any answers to their postings. This characteristic depicts someone who overthinks things. This is a person who is constantly concerned about what other people may say. As a consequence, they will be overly preoccupied with their social media postings and the reactions they will get.

"What if I'm the next?"

Without a doubt, we live in an unpredictable world. You can never be certain of what will happen tomorrow. This may affect how you see the unknown. There may be instances when you are afraid that the worst will come to you at any time. In this regard, you should be aware that such ideas are not uncommon. This is not to say that you should let such ideas consume you. You should learn how to govern your ideas now that you have some influence over them. Living in continual fear that you may trip at any moment is not a healthy way to live.

"My spouse hasn't phoned; they must be furious with me."

Anxiety may also harm your relationships in a variety of ways. Consider the following scenario: your spouse does not call you throughout the day. This might have occurred for a variety of reasons. Perhaps they were preoccupied or their phone's battery had died. Your anxious disposition, on the other hand, will lead you to believe that your spouse is unhappy with you for some reason. Having this view would only harm your lovely connection with your companion.

"Did I forget to close the door?"

Most individuals are too concerned with little details that they may have overlooked. You could, for example, ask yourself about your door, appliances, or light switches. You'll find your thoughts wandering as you consider whether or not the appliances were turned off. Repeating this will only increase your anxiousness.

Based on these common instances of worrying thoughts, it is obvious that overthinking may cause anxiety. The basic reality is that you can prevent yourself from thinking excessively. For example, your spouse forgetting to check on you might happen for a variety of reasons. Perhaps they are preoccupied at work and have their iPhones set to quiet mode. It's also possible that they're at a meeting.

As a result, there is no need for you to overthink things.

Accept the concept of accepting things as they are and without complicating them.

Triggers of Anxiety

You will be worried for a variety of reasons. Certain events, experiences, or feelings might exacerbate anxiety symptoms. These factors are known as anxiety triggers.

26

The following is a quick look at some of the most prevalent anxiety triggers.

Concerns About Health

Anxiety might be exacerbated by health worries. Typically, this occurs after a distressing medical diagnosis, such as chronic sickness or cancer. When suffering from a chronic ailment, it is typical for individuals to feel anxious about the course of their lives. The good news is that you may overcome your worry by altering how you think about and view your life. Living a busy life, for example, will keep you from focusing on the sickness. Instead, you will appreciate and enjoy what life has to offer.

Medications

Certain drugs might make you feel uneasy as well. This is because these drugs include active components that impact how one feels. Weight reduction drugs, birth control pills, and congestion treatments are examples of common medications that might induce anxiety.

Caffeine

Caffeine may aggravate or induce anxiety symptoms. Caffeine use should be reduced while suffering from a social anxiety disorder in particular.

Meal Skipping

There may be times when you feel uneasy as a result of skipping meals. This is caused by a dip in your blood sugar. Eating a well-balanced diet is suggested for a variety of reasons. It is beneficial to make an effort to eat a nutritious diet regularly to ensure that your body receives all of the nutrients it needs. Filling up on nutritious snacks helps to keep your blood sugar levels stable.

As a result, you are less likely to feel tense or irritated.

Negative Thoughts

Negative thinking will most likely contaminate your mind with sentiments of frustration. This suggests you are prone to be uneasy since you are too concerned with the worst-case scenario.

Concerns about money

With the current economic climate, it might be difficult to keep from worrying too much about your money. When you have obligations to pay and everything looks to be out of control, this becomes a huge issue. When dealing with financial issues, you might consider obtaining expert help.

Stress

For example, if you miss crucial deadlines, you will be concerned about the possibility of losing something vital. You may develop a dread of losing your work. This will, indeed, cause you a great deal of tension. Stress may have a detrimental influence on the quality of your sleep in certain situations. This aggravates your issue since anxiousness intensifies when you don't get enough sleep.

A Common Source of Stress Is Destructive Thinking

Negative thinking often leads to stress. When you continuously engage in negative self-talk, your subconscious mind will concentrate on it. Instead of dwelling on how awful things appear to follow you, it is important to recognize that such ideas may be detrimental to your emotional well-being. To understand how our thoughts cause stress, we must first understand how stress works.

How Does Stress Work?

Albert Ellis, a psychologist, devised the ABC model for understanding how stress operates. External events (A) do not elicit emotions, according to this concept (C). Beliefs (B) on the other hand, might elicit feelings.

This means that people's emotions are not immediately impacted by their surroundings, rather they are influenced by how they interpret what is happening around them.

Stressors, it may be argued, will always exist. For example, being caught in traffic is a typical occurrence. When you treat it negatively, it merely adds to your stress. In this sense, a gloomy attitude about traffic will induce worry and tension. Recognizing that you can influence how you think should assist you in realizing that you can easily avoid stress. So, why bother complaining about a traffic bottleneck when you know there's nothing you can do about it? To cope with such a scenario properly, you need to keep your mind occupied with anything else. While you wait for traffic to clear, listen to your favorite music. You may also listen to positive affirmations to ensure that your mind does not wander into negative thoughts.

Negative Self-Talk and Stress

The inner voice that speaks to you is known as self-talk. It becomes a make-or-break issue depending on how you employ self-talk. Positive self-talk will remind you of the fantastic things you are capable of doing. It will assist you in approaching life with hope. Bad self-talk, on the other hand, will bring negative energy into your life. You will be too concerned with the possibilities of all the horrible things that may happen to you.

Negative self-talk will not assist you to overcome any stress you may be experiencing. It aggravates the condition by making you feel more anxious.

Overthinking may harm your life in a variety of ways. Whether you're feeling nervous, stressed, or uninspired, it's all down to how you think. Thinking optimistically may help you attract nice things. Your ideas and emotions will always be subject to the law of attraction. It is through your ideas that you build the reality you want. Negative thinking leads to negative outcomes in your life. It will have various effects on your relationships, job life, and productivity. Instead of worrying about the future, spend your attention on what you can do now to make a better tomorrow. To be honest, your actions define your future. As a result, just thinking is insufficient. You must take action.

CHAPTER 3:

SCHEDULING THINKING TIME IS COVERED

Thinking and overthinking is not the same thing. The process of contemplating ideas, activities, and the like is known as thinking. It is the process of considering and deliberating about potential responses, behaviors, or ideas.

This act is critical and must be completed before reaching a choice. It may not be simple to regulate how, when, and what you think about, but it is quite doable with consistent practice. Practice will always lead to perfection.

As vital as thinking is, we must maintain control over what we think about, when we think about it, and how often we think about it. Allowing our thoughts to determine our thinking periods for us may be unhealthy since we will think at random. One method to avoid this is to schedule our thinking time at a more convenient time and adhere to it.

The daytime thinking process is preferable to the nighttime thinking process.

This is because our thoughts need rest, and the best time to rest the mind is at night when we sleep. Instead of keeping the mind active at night, utilize it during the day to think about and solve issues. This will allow you to have a good night's sleep. However, when it comes to dreaming about anything, the best time to do it is at night, rather than during the day when you need to focus.

Overthinking is a habit that develops over time, and changing it may be difficult. It is a comprehensive process that needs much more than just uttering words of commitment. You must be resolute in your activities, and one of those acts is to schedule thinking time.

Steps to "Schedule Thinking Time"

Scheduling thinking time may seem abstract to novices, but it improves with practice. There are many stages needed in doing this.

The actions or instructions you must follow are shown below. Do not discontinue the workout, no matter how ridiculous the next stages seem.

1. Choose a reflection process that corresponds to your tastes.

There are several methods to reflect on things, like keeping a journal, opening up to someone you can trust, going for a stroll, and many more. If one path does not seem to be feasible, try another while taking time to contemplate. When we have difficulties, we should not dismiss them with endless discussions about sports, news, and fashion. It's not a terrible thing to talk about these things, but it becomes an issue when they take away our time to contemplate.

2. Set aside time each day for pondering for a week.

Make it a habit to think at the same time every day for at least a week. For starters, it may be as little as 15 minutes, generally in the morning or throughout the day. Your thinking time should not be at night, right before you go to bed. This is because it will keep you awake and prevent you from getting the necessary amount of sleep.

3. Begin small.

You don't have to push yourself to perform one hour of contemplation time as a beginning if you can't keep to it. Scheduling time for thinking is a process. It is one thing to plan thinking time; it is quite another to keep to it. As a result, start small, 10 minutes or less if you can keep to the time.

4. Don't think about what you're going to think about.

Allow your meeting with yourself to be completely unexpected. Do not set aside the specific subject you want to think about and complete not arrange your time to coincide with days or times when you have a lot of work to do. This meeting should have no agenda; instead, let it be a moment of surprise for you and your ideas.

5. During that 15-30 minute period, jot down everything of your ideas.

Every day, decide that you will not stress or overthink the ideas you are going to have until the following thinking session. This will assist you in keeping your thoughts in control even after the thinking time has passed.

We may not always be aware of what is upsetting us, but with this phase, these issues will be disclosed. It is recommended that we strive to write down our ideas throughout our thinking hours. This will give us a better idea of what is upsetting us and what isn't. If your mind leads you to potential answers to your difficulties before your thinking time is over, that's OK, but if it doesn't, don't think about the problem beyond your thinking window.

6. In between periods of thought.

Do not ponder your ideas from the previous thought time to the next. This implies you should not think about your issues or solutions outside of your thinking time. This is not as simple as it seems; you will need to take conscious steps to prevent yourself from worrying about various concerns at random. Make a firm decision inside yourself to think about your concerns exclusively during your regular thinking period.

7. After the week, spend a few minutes reviewing everything you wrote down over the week.

Take some time after each week to reflect on your ideas from the previous week. Take note of reoccurring ideas, thoughts that stopped arriving after a time, thoughts that continued to come, changes in your thoughts, and every element of your thinking patterns. Consider these insights when you narrow down the top 10 on your list.

8. After completing this task for one week, consider doing it again.

Remember that practice makes perfect, that a habit does not establish overnight, but that persistence makes it happen. If you repeat the above procedures regularly, you will gradually learn that you have control over your ideas, including where, when, and how often you think.

It is one method of coping with life's uncertainty. This life is full of hazards; we can't anticipate what will happen in the next 30 minutes, and this has led many individuals to vow to be concerned about everything. However, instead of focusing on all of life's sources of anxiety, you may focus on the ones you can solve and let go of the ones you can't.

Teach your thoughts to stay calm and tranquil in stressful times.

Consider it carefully.

The bulk of us has a habit of overthinking circumstances over which we have little control. To be honest, thinking about these things is just meaningless. I highly advise you to begin thinking effectively.

For example, you may have been hoping for a promotion at work.

You must realize that earning that promotion is TOTALLY in the hands of your employer, regardless of the additional credentials you provide on your CV. In this scenario, useless thinking is a waste of time and mental energy worrying whether he would advance you or not.

On the contrary, your thoughts should be focused on what you need to achieve to be considered for a promotion. You may need to improve your abilities, get another credential, or demonstrate more commitment to your profession. Whatever the scenario may be, think in terms of producing outcomes rather than lamenting!

I agree that it is difficult to overcome certain thought habits, but liberating yourself from these patterns may unleash your resourcefulness, and I have provided some methods to assist you to liberate yourself from these thinking patterns.

Experiment with hypotheses. For each new scenario, some assumptions must be made.

You should put these ideas to the test for a larger range of chances and prospects.

You assume that you cannot afford to buy a property or even pay a deposit, therefore you do not buy the house. Put that idea to the test by assessing your assets to determine whether their value can earn you that property in exchange. I mean, even if you don't have the money in cash or your account, don't take a big step just on a hunch. Ask yourself what you can do to acquire the money, and it may not seem so difficult.

This is the problem. You may be shocked to discover that when you express things differently, you become more creative. This can only be accomplished by keeping an open mind and approaching the problem from many angles. Try to look at it objectively, without emotion, so you can address the situation rationally. Ask yourself all of the difficult but necessary questions, and it will be simpler to devise fresh solutions to the problems.

Enterprises that owned shipments lost their goods on wagons in the mid-1950s. Even though they subsequently attempted to focus on faster production and development as well as more efficient ships, they are still unable to resolve the difficulties. Soon after, a professional revised the definition of the problem, talking about it in a completely different manner. He said that the new problem should be analyzing strategies for the industry to begin reducing costs. This shift in emphasis opened the door to new techniques. Every aspect, except shipments and storage, was discussed. This new approach eventually resulted in what is known as a container ship and roll on wagon/crate.

Turn your mind around. When you're stuck and can't figure out how to solve a problem, consider inverting it or flipping it. Take a look at it from the opposite side. Consider how to cause the problem and worsen the situation rather than how to solve it. This reversal tactic will provide new ideas about how to approach the case. When you flip the situation upside down, you could receive some clarity.

Communicate in a variety of ways. We don't always have to utilize our spoken logical medium when confronted with an issue, which is fairly typical of us. We are much too intelligent to restrict our thinking powers.

Use several approaches to express your concerns. Don't be too concerned about addressing the issue at this stage. Simply put, eloquent. Many different thought patterns may be generated by diverse persons using various modes of articulation to birth new ideas.

Join the dots. Most of the most successful ideas don't appear to be planned; they simply happen. It might be anything random you saw or heard that inspires you to come up with that brilliant idea. Several instances back this concept, including Apple, Newton, and others.

You may be wondering why we are so impacted by randomness; it is because this unpredictability triggers our brains into new thinking patterns. As a result, you may take advantage of this and join the separated portions.

Look for impulse in unexpected areas and attempt to connect the fragmented components of the case and the impetus. The following are some methods for expanding the network:

Use irrelevant advice. Consider selecting a word at random from the dictionary and attempting to build a network between your problem and the term.

Associate the likely notions. Put a specific word on the paper, and then write anything that comes to mind on the same page. Then attempt to connect them with a network.

You may, for example, choose a random picture and see if you can connect it to the case.

Pick up anything, anything, and think about how it can aid your case by asking yourself important questions to discover what the object has as a characteristic that can help turn the situation around.

Change your perspective. If you desire new ideas, you may need to modify your perspective on the problem, since holding a specific point of view will only result in the same related concepts over time.

Inquire about the thoughts of others. People are so diverse that we all handle an issue in our unique manner. As a result, solicit other people's perspectives and recommended a course of action in the matter. It may be your kid, a friend, a customer, your spouse, or even a random stranger with a whole different lifestyle and possibly a very different attitude on life.

Participate in a game. You may try to see things through the eyes of a billionaire, or imagine what Obama would do if you were him.

Any prominent person you chose has a distinct personality; thus, evaluate these characteristics and utilize them to approach the topic from a different perspective. For example, if you take on the position of a millionaire, you may be required to demonstrate their characteristics as well while planning. Extravagance and adventure are characteristics of this industry. Someone like Tiger Woods, on the other hand, is more likely to demonstrate perfectionism, perseverance, and meticulous attention to every detail of the case.

The facultative design you create may help you develop a positive attitude, which will increase your inventive thinking.

When you see yourself sliding into the overthinking mode, redirect your thoughts toward efficient thinking and eliminate any nonproductive thinking.

CHAPTER 4:

SET TIME LIMITS FOR MAKING DECISIONS

Everything about us is the result of our decisions. Friendships, health, and even our profession, as well as everything else that makes us who we are today, are determined by our ability or inability to make decisions, as well as the choices we have previously made. Having stated that, it is regrettable that many individuals continue to struggle with decision-making.

Even if everything else seems to be going well for us, when the chips are down and the time comes to make that critical decision, we curl up. It simply seems so difficult to make a decision and stick to it.

Every day, we live by the many choices we must make, no matter how little or large. That is the essence of life. We will be able to make greater progress if we can break down these large choices into smaller ones.

The adage "the best choice is no decision at all" is virtually always incorrect. Indecisive people are more prone to be dominated by their life rather than the other way around. You may not be as self-sufficient as you would want if you lack control over your life as a consequence of indecisiveness; thus, you must learn to be determined and take command of your life.

The greatest method to kickstart your overthinking habit is to choose with a strong desire to do it right and plenty of time to do so. The whole process of deliberating on the best course of action, examining all of your alternatives while taking your time, is an invitation to overthinking things. Setting a time restriction for yourself is the most efficient strategy to break the habit. It is best to establish a span restriction depending on the severity or size of the choice. When the limit is reached, stop any further examination and just choose an option, act on it, and continue.

The goal of this advice is to eliminate the possibility of overthinking and to force action within your time frame. It's simple: start time yourself as soon as you begin the analytical process to conclude. Because you are cognizant of time, your examination of the benefits and drawbacks will be briefer. In truth, this procedure is quite straightforward.

If you take too long to make decisions, this advice is exactly what you need. You may set the timer to 1 minute, 5 minutes, or any amount in between.

How to Set Decision-Making Time Limits

Set a limit to the number of options you have. When attempting to make a choice, restrict your possibilities to no more than three, rather than leaving them broad, huge, and endless.

Parkinson's Theorem (set a bar on your time). When you establish a time limit, you work less and stress you're brainless, and there just isn't enough time to work your brain out. Work will only be moved to make the most of the available time.

Keep your thoughts to a minimum. Three people's views are sufficient to assist you with your analysis. Don't confuse yourself; individuals disagree; the fewer contradicting viewpoints you hear, the simpler it will be to reach a decision.

41

Reminder: if you find yourself asking for other people's views regularly, it might mean that you aren't sure what you want, or that you don't want it at all. Getting a second or third opinion now and then can help you confirm a decision you've already made.

The napkin method. Because you can't accomplish much on a napkin, it's ideal to sketch down your strategy first, and you'll see that just the most crucial details will be sketched.

Maintain an optimistic attitude. When you learn to recognize the positive in every choice and decision, you will be able to accept the outcomes without regret. You make the choice, and then you learn from it.

The plank walk method. Make a promise to yourself to do something you despise or would rather avoid if you don't choose within the time limit. Either you go all the way or you don't go at all.

CHAPTER 5:

PUTTING YOUR THOUGHTS TO THE TEST

You must first retrain your brain to cease overthinking. Fortunately, there are several exercises and activities available to help you modify your thinking.

Now that you know a bit about overthinking and when you are on the edge of falling into that deep vortex of limitless bad feelings, you can begin to get rid of it completely, and you can begin by confronting your ideas before they get out of control.

Before You Start

Here are some things you should know before you start fighting your negative beliefs, so you don't become too startled or overwhelmed by anything that happens.

1. You should be aware that confronting your views may seem odd, even forced at first. However, with a little practice, it will begin to seem natural and realistic.

2. To gain confidence in thinking challenging, practice concepts that are not as unpleasant and allow a little more flexibility. It is also a good idea to use this approach while you are still feeling neutral and not overburdened by your thoughts. Attempting to practice thought challenging after a very difficult and unpleasant day would be too much to expect of oneself.

3. It's a good idea to note down your replies the first couple of times you attempt thinking-provoking. When novices attempt it in their brains, they often wind up with their ideas spinning around in circles, which intensifies their thoughts and may lead them to slide into overthinking.

4. Another advantage of taking notes is that if a similar idea arises in the future, you may go to your notes to see how you responded to it.

5. You may practice with a family member or a friend you know won't judge you. Practicing with another person may benefit you by throwing light on the blind spots in your thinking, or they may provide you with alternative perspectives that you may find valuable.

6. When you initially begin practicing thought challenging, you should concentrate on a single idea rather than a succession of them. Instead of thinking, "It's very evident that my employers believed I screwed up the project," break your ideas down into smaller, simpler words, and then confront these assumptions one by one.

You will simply confuse yourself if you begin confronting a slew of concepts at once.

44

7. Once you've finished going through a couple of thought-provoking topics, do something to divert your attention. This will allow you some time to clear your head.

Now that you know what to anticipate, here are some of the most popular thought-provoking exercises you can attempt right now.

Take a step back and evaluate the situation.

Here's a situation you may have encountered: you get the impression that your employer is purposefully ignoring you. You believe that the reason your boss did not welcome you this morning is that you did something wrong and that he is planning to fire you shortly. Typically, these kinds of ideas drive your mind to overthink and cause you to lose sleep, which causes you to be less efficient at work, which leads to you being fired; in short, overthinking issues cause them to become self-fulfilling prophecies.

You can, on the other hand, regulate it better if you take a step back and assess your ideas before your busy brain blows them out of proportion. Next, consider what you might do to avoid being fired, such as raising your productivity or learning a new skill that will help you perform your work better.

You have disrupted your train of negative thinking before it even had a chance to acquire speed in only a few minutes.

Make a list of them all.

Another method for challenging negative ideas before they cause you to overthink is to write them all down on a piece of paper. When you write down the things that annoy you, they take on a more concrete shape, which allows you to reanalyze them more rationally. If you want to take it a step further, you might start keeping a thinking notebook.

What exactly is a thinking journal or diary?

A thought diary differs from typical journaling in that it has a framework that must be followed to make evaluating your ideas simpler. In a thinking journal, for example, you do not begin an entry with "Dear Diary" or any other form of it; rather, the entries resemble a ledger.

You create a thinking journal by dividing the paper into two columns and labeling them as follows:

Antecedent - These are the events that occurred throughout the day that prompted you.

Beliefs – These are your feelings about the items listed in the first column.

Consequences – These are the events that occurred as a result of your thoughts.

This is why a thought diary is sometimes referred to as an ABC journal.

Here's an example of how to write a thought journal entry. You get concerned because you have an approaching payment that you must pay; this is your consequence. You mention in the second column that you were concerned that you would not be able to meet your deadline.

After a while of writing in your thoughts notebook, you may notice that the triggers are typically unrelated to the ideas that caused you to worry. Thoughts simply happen, and the triggers that brought them up may or may not be linked to them; thoughts are fickle in that manner.

You may then put something like, "I took an aspirin to get rid of the headache that I sensed was coming" in the consequences section.

Every Sunday evening, you may go through your submissions and consider what you could have done better. For example, instead of taking aspirin, you might have just strolled around the park to clear your thoughts, or at the very least eat an apple or anything to keep your headache from worsening. You might also phone your utility provider and explain that you may be a bit late on the payment, but that you will pay, and ask if they would waive the late fines. Your thought notebook will assist you in making sense of your jumbled ideas by setting them down on paper for easy analysis. This quiz might help you understand your less-than-ideal coping abilities and why you wind up making decisions that have unfavorable outcomes for you. You may modify your future outcomes by restating and reanalyzing your previous ideas and making the required modifications with the aid of a thought diary.

The Advantages of Keeping a Thought Journal

Writing in a thought journal/diary assists you in identifying the factors that cause you to overthink. When you write down your ideas, you can quickly determine whether they are serious worries or merely illogical. Thought diaries assist you in recalling how you acted at the moment you were prompted into overthinking, and over time, you will begin to recognize patterns in the way you think.

When you become aware of your current thinking patterns, you will be able to modify not just your behavior, but also your thoughts. When you sense bad ideas creeping in, you may practice mindfulness (more on this later) and just observe and recognize them until they go. You do not have to act by your ideas; you may just disregard them and go about your business. It is much better to write "I disregarded the idea of..." rather than "I went to the bar and drank a few beers to make myself forget," and if you see that you are doing the same thing practically every day, your thought journal is effective.

Make it a habit to keep a thinking diary.

You may use a little notepad, a stack of papers, or anything else on which you can write and keep private. No one else should be aware of the existence of this diary, save you and your therapist (if you are seeing one); no one else should have access to your inner thoughts.

If you do not want to utilize the usual technique, you may create a secret document on your smartphone or laptop. Gradually, you will become aware of when you are about to spiral into overthinking and will be able to stop yourself from going any farther.

Negative feelings, such as those that destroy your confidence, may generally lead to severe depression, making you feel inexplicably lonely and hopeless, and they will tear you apart on the inside.

Writing assists you in overcoming self-destructive thinking. It is an art form that may help you express your deepest emotions and ideas.

Writing down your sentiments on paper allows you to openly express your thoughts and ideas on what occurred throughout the day and the impact it had on your life. You're not simply putting things on paper; you're essentially removing all of these unpleasant ideas from your head, and with them, all of the negativity that accompanied them.

Take up a New Interest

If you've always wanted to learn to play the piano, guitar, ukulele, or any other musical instrument, why not start today? Do you wish to improve your drawing, calligraphy, or painting skills?

Attend courses or watch video tutorials online. You may also spend an hour or so playing your favorite video games. A pastime not only provides you with a creative outlet, but it also enables you to produce something with your hands, it helps you to think independently, and, most significantly, it provides you with an escape from your negative thoughts.

Whenever your thoughts begin to overwhelm you, get out your hobby equipment and immerse yourself in the activity.

Lose yourself in the skills, coordination, concentration, and repetition required by your hobby. Concentrate your thoughts on the comfort or challenge provided by your chosen interest, and let it drive away all of the anxieties that used to cause your overthinking.

Worries Can Be Removed Through Meditation

Meditation might genuinely help you divert your attention away from the things that are bothering you. Indeed, guided meditation may help you reset your mind, leaving you unburdened and rejuvenated, ready to face any problems that may arise.

Meditation is not the same as mindfulness; the latter is a spontaneous method that may be used anywhere and at any time.

Meditation, in its purest form, should be performed as often as possible in a quiet, tranquil, and pleasant setting.

Here are a few meditation techniques to try. Give them all a shot and pick the one with whom you connect the most.

1. Concentrated breathing

Breathing is an automatic movement of the body, which means that you do not need to instruct your body to breathe; it simply occurs.

You may, however, convert your breathing into a sort of meditation simply by paying attention to each breath you take.

You take long, slow, deep breaths in focused breathing meditation; breaths so deep that you fill your belly with air as well. To practice this type of meditation, you must clear your mind of all thoughts and concentrate solely on your breathing. This is particularly useful when you see that your thoughts are beginning to spiral out of control.

This procedure, however, may not be suitable for persons suffering from respiratory conditions such as asthma, as well as certain cardiac conditions.

2. Body Scanning

This method combines breath focus and muscular relaxation methods. Begin by taking a few deep breaths, then concentrate your attention on one portion of your body, or a group of muscles, after you feel a little more relaxed. For example, concentrate on the fingers on your left foot, noticing all of the feelings that each toe is experiencing, and then mentally releasing any physical tension there. Then, concentrate on another group of muscles.

A body scan not only relaxes you but also increases your awareness of your mind and body. However, if you have just had surgery that has had a substantial impact on your body image, or if you have body dysmorphic disorder, this procedure may be more harmful than beneficial.

3. Meditation with a Guide

This technique necessitates the creation of soothing scenery, locations, or experiences that may aid in your relaxation. If you're having trouble coming up with scenarios for your guided meditation sessions, you may utilize one of the numerous free applications accessible online.

Guided visualization is fantastic since all you have to do is follow the directions of the smooth-spoken teacher and you'll be fine.

This strategy is most suited for those who have recurring intrusive thoughts.

4. Meditation for Mindfulness

This technique requires just that you sit comfortably and concentrate on the present moment without straying to your unpleasant thoughts of the past or future. This type is now gaining popularity, owing to its ability to treat patients suffering from anxiety, chronic pain, and despair.

Yoga, Tai Chi, or Qui Gong are all good options.

These three ancient arts may not appear to be related, but they all combine rhythmic breathing with various postures and body movements. Because you must concentrate on your breathing while doing various postures, these exercises are great at diverting your attention away from your negative thoughts. Furthermore, these exercises can help you improve your flexibility, balance, and core strength. However, if you have a severe or painful disease that precludes you from doing anything physically strenuous, these activities may not be suitable for you. However, you may still ask your doctor whether you can do these exercises; he may be able to suggest a reputable physical therapist or gym that can assist you. Now, if your doctor feels that doing these exercises is a poor idea, take his advice and hunt for another alternative.

5. Chants/Prayers Repetitive

This approach is appropriate for those who have short attention spans and have difficulty concentrating on their breath.

For this approach, you concentrate on your breath while reciting a brief prayer or perhaps a line or two from a prayer. If you are religious or a highly spiritual person, this strategy may appeal to you more.

If you are not religious or do not believe in any religion, you may substitute positive affirmations or lines from your favorite poetry for the prayers/chants.

It is much preferable to test as many as possible before settling on the one or ones that work best for you. It is also advised that you practice these strategies for at least 20 minutes every day for the greatest effects, however even a few minutes might aid.

The longer and more often you practice these strategies, however, the higher the advantages and stress reduction.

CHAPTER 6:

DECLUTTER YOUR ENVIRONMENT

Did you see this one coming (even before you saw the table of contents)? You're probably wondering what a tidy house has to do with my overthinking. Well, the answer is—quite a bit!

Our surroundings have a huge impact on us in ways that are not always evident or immediately recognized. An employee who is required to execute their work in an unpleasant environment will surely underperform compared to another employee who is required to perform their jobs in a comfortable, clean environment.

Consider how you feel after a thorough cleaning of your house (which you should have done at least once or twice!). Isn't it nice to glance around and see a tidy house? It boosts the spirits and clears the mind in the same way as the actual area before you has been cleansed. The clutter in our homes might be precisely proportionate to the mess in our brains at times. So, let's get this party started!

It's critical to remember that this isn't another one-size-fits-all answer. When it comes to house organization, everyone has a distinct personality, style, and degree of comfort, and having a spotless home does not immediately ensure a significant increase in productivity.

The truth is that cleaning your house can only benefit your mental health, so why not make the effort?

If you live with a spouse, loved one, or roommate, you should discuss this idea before just moving or tossing stuff away! If it is a shared living area, it should be a collaborative endeavor. Your living partners will almost certainly agree after you express what you want to accomplish!

But first, let's look at why it's important to reorganize and declutter one's home.

Hoarding and disorder, on the other hand, are strong indicators that certain things in the mind need to be sorted up and arranged. Our physical environment is often a mirror of our mental surroundings.

Take a look around your house or personal living area. How do you feel about the way it appears now? Is it making you sad?

Overwhelmed? When we feel like we have no control over our lack of organization, it can spiral out of control. Attempting to treat the outward impacts of overthinking, stress, worry, or depression before dealing with the inside causes is always useless. If you don't address the thought process and bad habits, even if you clean up your space, it will most likely return to its previous state within weeks or even days.

If you've seen the TV show Hoarders, you'll know that a hoarder's habit is often motivated by an emotional attachment to a traumatic event in their lives. If this describes you and you've made measures to strengthen your mental processes, you're in an excellent position to start thinking about your living environment.

Keep in mind that this procedure is mostly for those of us who need aid with a job that has become somewhat onerous. You may have no trouble keeping your house tidy and clean, which is fantastic. For those of you who fit this description, my recommendation is to consider incorporating another feature into your house that promotes relaxation and comfort. Perhaps a tiny plant that you can tend to throughout the week, or a plaque with a motivating saying that you can hang on the wall and view every day. Any tiny reminder you can give yourself each day as you continue on your quest may be a tremendous confidence booster.

But, if you're one of those who feel overwhelmed by the enormity of the work ahead of you, let's start at the beginning.

The first step is to take a step back and understand that you will need to take one step at a time. Don't glance around the home and feel overwhelmed, as if you'll never be able to order anything. You should begin with one room, preferably the smallest.

Take a look around the room and consider how and why this material came to be there. Is it enough to make you feel uneasy or sad just looking at your belongings? If this is the case, it must be addressed.

Because different items will be destined for different futures, you'll need a few different boxes or bags. It may be beneficial to have someone there whom you trust to assist you in determining which is which.

One box should be labeled "donate," and these are the items in reasonable condition that you no longer need. It's not a question of whether you'll find a use for it in the future. If it's been sitting for months and you haven't touched it, chances are you don't need it. Please pass it on.

You'll also need a garbage bag. When we've developed negative attachment emotions, it can be painful to let go of things we've held on to for a long time. Consider your goals for decluttering your environment. Weigh the significance of this or that thing about what you want to achieve in your life. If the emotional response to that thing falls into the category of an impediment in your life path, you must get rid of it. If you can't bear the thought of trashing or donating anything, maybe someone you know can keep it for you. Holding on to it, on the other hand, will only serve to keep you back.

A third, fourth, and maybe fifth box should be there for items that you want to retain but need to arrange. Perhaps there is something in one room that would make more sense in another, and so forth. Before you begin rearranging these items, you should get everything off the floor or out of the room so that you may thoroughly vacuum or sweep the floors after dusting the corners of the ceiling, ceiling fan, and blinds and wiping down the tables or other surfaces around the room. It will be much more pleasurable to arrange and redesign the area after it has been well cleaned!

This is the procedure you will use for the remainder of your space. Take a break if things get too much. You don't have to finish everything in one day. Continue to remind yourself what a significant and significant step you are taking to improve your life.

Areas such as the kitchen and bathroom may require the most work.

Remember to remove and arrange objects before attempting to clean surfaces, as this will simply annoy you and lead to a poor level of cleaning. If you can afford it, you might think about hiring a professional cleaning service to come in and clean just a few of the most difficult rooms in the house. Don't be ashamed if they're really bad. Just make sure you've removed and trashed anything that needs to be moved out of the way. Many services will provide excellent introductory rates to new customers and for one-time services.

There are several ways for getting rid of goods you no longer need or use. Donation boxes can be found in stores such as Goodwill and the Salvation Army. If you have baby clothing or toys, maybe there is a church where you can give them. Another possibility is to have a yard sale. Make a small profit on those items and rest assured that they will be put to good use by someone else.

Minimalism

I'd like to offer an idea and way of living that has gained popularity in recent years. I'm not saying that everyone who reads this book should immediately get rid of 90% of their belongings and adopt this lifestyle, but I do believe that talking about it will open your mind to the possibilities and positive mindset that minimalism fosters.

Minimalism is a straightforward notion. Practitioners simplify their lives to the necessities to live the most simple and sustainable lifestyle possible.

The belief systems and motivations for adopting a minimalist lifestyle differ from person to person. Many people share some views and values, such as caring for their ecosystems and reducing their personal "ecological footprints" on the planet. Many practitioners are young people who have "burned out" (sound familiar?) in our contemporary economic rat race that is profession and career and simply switched to an extreme concentration after discovering they didn't like the path in which they were traveling.

A shift to minimalism is a departure from the immensely materialistic, hectic, and stressful lifestyle of never-ending wealth. It is a rejection of all that surrounds you and becomes a cage and addiction for more. When we remove items that have emotionally bound us, like a hoarder who chooses to make a change and get rid of superfluous possessions, a big surge of liberation and clarity awaits us. Minimalism is possibly the most straightforward analogy for how what's going on inside our heads can correspond to what's going on in our immediate surroundings. It's almost like a spiritual rite in which you commit to maintaining a mentality of clarity and present every day for the rest of your life. The simple way of life around you serves as a constant reminder of the mental shifts that have occurred.

Money is, of course, one of the most powerful addictions in modern society. If I had to guess, I'd say financial concerns were probably near the top of your initial list of overburdened thoughts. And it makes sense, doesn't it? Today, it is difficult to exist without money. And everything becomes more expensive as we age and accumulate more possessions. Purchases that were designed to provide us with ease and independence, such as our autos, turn out to be money pits. Some people believe they require the largest SUV on the market to accommodate their urban lifestyles without children...okay, I'm getting off track. But do you see where I'm going with this?

This society that demands more, more, more leads to nothing but emptiness, uncertainty, misery, and an overburdened mind swayed by everyone attempting to tell us what we need. All of our problems would vanish if we only had the most recent version of the iPhone! I'd feel prettier and have a simpler life if I changed my hair and got highlights! I'll be richer and happier if I get that job and work more hours! The list could go on and on.

You now have a better understanding of the mindset that underpins minimalism. It's not just about getting rid of things to save money, though that's a nice benefit. It's about clearing your mind of the clutter that life throws at you—things that are wrongly thought to provide things that can only be discovered in human interactions and connections, introspection, creativity, belief systems, and so on. Money can never buy happiness. Happiness is an ephemeral state that arises spontaneously from personal life experiences that rarely have anything to do with money.

So, how far does this minimalism thing go? If you're interested, there's a whole new world of what is known as "small houses," which are becoming more popular. Now, I'm sure this is much too severe for you at this time, but it's still an interesting issue to look into if you're inquisitive.

Tiny houses are just that: very, very little. They may be as tiny as your bathroom and have just the most basic of contemporary conveniences. You have a place to sleep, a place to make modest meals, perhaps a tiny location to keep a very, very few items, and...all! that's But, when you think about it, it's not all that unlike RV living, which is another popular option to escape the pressures and financial strains of contemporary life.

(An RV isn't much more than a little house, but it's transportable!)

The premise is that we do not need all of the things that marketers tell us we do. We can genuinely survive on a very modest diet of simple, wholesome, environmentally friendly food and the delight of being with people we care about. Applying this approach to your own life may help you see how little and meaningless many of your previous issues and anxieties were. We are conditioned to feel an emptiness and the desire to fill it with things.

When those things begin to clutter our homes and personal environments, we can see a direct correlation between this environment and the one inside our minds. Decluttering your home and making room for a new beginning is invaluable in assisting with the effort of decluttering your mind. Take the time you need to finish this important step, and you'll be ready to build on the new and improved you in no time.

Once you've made efforts in decluttering your house, you will find you are not only able to move more freely around your area, but that your thinking becomes clearer, too! All of these phases are there for a purpose, and they will all work together to benefit you as you grow.

When you've arrived at this point, take a big breath and gaze about your house. This is your new blank canvas on which to paint your life the way you've always imagined it.

The next phase in our trip will be to focus on how to develop excellent habits that will promote your ongoing win over information overload and overthinking. Many individuals never get to visit this location, so give yourself a huge pat on the back. This could also be a good time to reflect on the people in your life with whom you have the most in common. Do you have a loved one or a close friend who appears to be suffering from overthinking and information overload in the same way you have?

Perhaps you could find a partner to assist you in developing good habits. You never know, you might be able to significantly improve another person's life along the way!

CHAPTER 7:

THOUGHT MODIFICATION EXAMPLES

Three separate instances of people using thought modification to replace bad behaviors with good ones are shown below. You'll note that, although the specifics vary from instance to case, the formula remains consistent. Individuals in each case have an unhealthy tendency to overthinking, which causes them to seek solace via harmful behaviors such as drinking, smoking, and overeating.

Examine how each scenario employs parts of positive thinking, purposeful thinking, and behavior modification to see if you can identify each. Take note of if any of these applications stimulate thoughts for how you may use positive and purposeful thought as you seek to eliminate overthinking and perhaps other non-productive behaviors.

Example #1: The Person Who Gives Up Drinking

In this example, the guy has admitted that he has a propensity to overthink, which leads to him drinking to cope with the stress and worry he experiences. This person suffers from paranoia and self-doubt; he is often concerned that people think the worst of him and do not want him around. Sometimes he will concentrate on ideas that tell him his friends adore him and no one is condemning him, while other times he will obsess over made-up dreams that people are gossiping behind his back about how much they despise him and all the foolish things he does.

The person becomes aware that both versions of the narrative exist in his head. He has a tale in his head about how his friends adore him for being himself, just as much as he has a story about how they despise him.

Sometimes he focuses all of his attention on one version of the narrative, and other times he focuses all of his attention on the other.

When this person's mind is already focused on thoughts and emotions of self-doubt, self-criticism, and dread, more concepts like it join them. When he has been submitting himself to self-criticism and self-cruelty for the previous 30 minutes, it is much simpler to get drawn into the emotional misery of a tale about how everyone hates him. With a lot of velocities, this person's train is heading in the wrong direction.

When these negative ideas come together, they amplify the individual's tension, uncertainty, and anxiety. When the person needs respite from these agonizing thoughts, he starts to drink. Nothing out of the ordinary has occurred, but the guy has noticed that he dislikes the way alcohol makes his body feel in the morning. He dislikes the loss of attention and concentration he has after a night of binge drinking. He dislikes depending on a chemical to provide relief. Most of all, he dislikes the early overthinking that drives him to spiral out of control with bad thoughts and images.

The most difficult portion has been completed. The guy has acknowledged that this behavior pattern is no longer beneficial to him; rather, it is harmful and inconvenient. The person knows that since the majority of his problems have formed as a result of harmful thinking patterns, this must be the spot to begin the healing and rejuvenation process. He begins the process of development with his ideas, which are the foundation of all action and reality.

The person examines and chooses a replacement behavior to lower the frequency of drinking and replace it with something beneficial. For a time, drinking was a method to experience relief from tension and to be free of oppressive ideas. As a result, the person chooses a substitute behavior that will similarly provide relief and a brief escape. This person enjoys making music and playing the drums. He hasn't had the attention or energy to play recently as a result of the drinking routine he's developed.

When he does play, though, he feels as if he is in his universe; the troubles of reality, as well as all the paranoid and oppressive ideas, vanish. Playing a couple of his favorite songs on the drums helps him relieve even more tension than drinking does. He feels energetic and enthusiastic once he finishes playing the drums. He is considering recording music and is spending more time in his basement music studio. He'd want to substitute drinking with drumming. When he gets home at night, he changes his schedule somewhat. Instead of pouring a drink while still dressed for work, he will change into some comfy clothes and go directly to his music studio. Instead of the first whiskey of the night, he vents his anger on the drums, banging out whatever feels best and what he wants to perform.

The guy has developed a few tactics and mental exercises that help him regulate and discard unwanted ideas that make him feel awful. He's also chosen a substitute behavior. He now adds another crucial component for conditioning, the punishment and reward. In this situation, the penalty and reward will be monetary.

The guy chooses to alter his usual routine merely a little, but with significant benefits. He'll take the same route home every night. He'll even keep stopping at the same shop where he buys alcohol.

Instead of buying alcohol, he will deposit $25 into his savings account using his phone or an ATM at the shop.

Every day, he takes the time to pause and watch the balance in his savings account grow. He is aware of how he feels. He takes a moment to relish that sensation before running into the shop for anything else he may want before returning home to change into comfy clothes and go to his studio.

If he has transferred the $25 a day instead of spending it on whiskey at the end of the week, he rewards himself with a shopping excursion to the music store that money. If he makes a mistake and purchases alcohol, he must donate $50 to a charity chosen by the app, which helps children afford instruments and music instruction. He believes he will be less likely to make a mistake since the whiskey will cost him three times as much. He also believes that a shopping spree is a good motivator since he has a wish list of equipment.

All of these activities are conscious or subconscious confirmations to himself that he does not have to dwell on the negative exaggerations and that he does have control over his thoughts and actions. He is pleased with himself for learning to replace bad behavior and, in the meanwhile, he is reaping several perks and advantages as a result of doing so. Soon, the individual's train has changed course and gained such great velocity that life is pleasurable and a poor coping technique such as alcohol is no longer wanted.

Example #2: The Person Who Quits Smoking

In this situation, the person has recently developed a tendency to overthink, overanalyze, and self-criticism as a result of work-related stress. She has lately been pushed at work to demonstrate that she is qualified for the job she desires. Others in the firm are also interested in this role.

The rivalry has gotten tough, and she feels as though everything she does is being analyzed under a microscope, so she must perform flawlessly. She enjoys the challenge and wants the job; she doesn't mind the hard work, but she continues to overwork herself to tiredness and self-doubt, draining all of her creative growth and enthusiasm. That energy is then utilized to continually worry or picture bad situations.

She tries to recollect a time when she felt as tense and nervous, and when she does, she recalls smoking a cigarette as a means to deal with her stress and agony. This sends her to the shop to get a pack of cigarettes. She's on her way home with one. It's all too familiar. It relieves some of the tension she is now experiencing; she gets a sense of calm as a result of this encounter.

She soon enjoys a cigarette on her way home from work. On her way into the workplace, she begins to have them. It won't be long before

She's outside in the smoking pit with all the other smokers taking a smoke break. It isn't long until she buys a carton of cigarettes, something she promised herself she would never do again.

However, this person is now experiencing health issues. She can't breathe as well as she used to, and she sometimes experiences shortness of breath when she shouldn't. She's coughing even more. Her throat is inflamed. Worse, the early sense of calm she regained has disappeared. She is now largely left with an expensive, harmful habit that no longer produces a pleasant consequence. It simply allows her a few additional minutes to stew over unpleasant thoughts in her head while she's on a smoke break.

This person has noticed that negative and compulsive over-analysis and over-thinking of recent job issues are impeding her achievement and prompting her to create undesirable behaviors as coping methods. She has resolved to alter this mental pattern, adapt it, and substitute the bad behavior of smoking.

This person makes more major alterations to her routine to replace her harmful smoking behavior. She determines that she does not need a direct substitute for smoking; that is, she does not require a replacement habit to perform every hour.

She hadn't smoked in years and didn't need to do anything every hour to feel better, and she'd want to go back to that.

Instead, she intends to treat herself to a massage at the gym. Her gym membership allows her to use the hydro massage bed and massage chairs, but she never finds the time. She goes to the gym every other day and wants to reward herself with a 10-minute massage every time she does not smoke between visits.

This is not her sole strategy for overcoming her unfavorable smoking habits. This person has also sought the assistance of a trained hypnotist. If she decides to smoke, the hypnotist has used an operant conditioning technique that adds an immediate and unpleasant response to the smoking experience. When this person needs more reinforcements when she feels like smoking a cigarette, operant conditioning will come in handy.

The hypnotist's addition to the smoking experience is an unpleasant taste in the mouth. The hypnotist induces a trance and takes the client through the sensation of smoking, but in this imagined situation, the individual is pushed to recognize the already awful taste of smoking. The hypnotist elaborates and exaggerates on that sensation, persuading the subject that it is the most revolting flavor she has ever tasted. He associates this event with a series of profoundly unpleasant sensory signals, prompting the person to recall the smell of truck stop temporary restrooms when she smokes up.

All of these unpleasant sensory experiences are associated with smoking behavior, and this person eventually finds herself unable to even smell an unlit cigarette without her stomach twisting. She'll be in the massage chairs in a couple of days and hasn't smoked since. She feels more interested at work now that she has quit smoking, and she does not feel as if people are gossiping about her behind her back as she would when she would go out for a smoke break. She treats herself to massage equipment at the gym regularly and utilizes that time to intentionally practice healthy and positive thinking activities. She sees it as a full-service gym membership where she can work out both her body and her head.

Example #3: The Person Who Substitutes Overeating

In this scenario, the person has just lately begun living on her own. As a consequence, she has recently adopted some bad eating habits.

Because she is the only one eating, she is less likely to take the time to ensure her meals are balanced and appropriate. Furthermore, after a string of stressful days, she believes she is deserving of the meals she desires.

Overthinking will become a habit for her as a result of little disagreements. On the way home, she has a little encounter with traffic, and that is all she can think about. She keeps returning her attention to the situation. Was she in error? Shouldn't she have said anything else? How dare the other drivers point the finger at her! She comes up with a fantastic comeback that is 20 minutes too late. She's curious about the driver's issue.

She ruminates over it. She makes up all sorts of tales about injustice and wrongdoing to get herself stirred up.

She is hungry, weary, and agitated by the time she comes home after all of her overthinking. She orders delivery or goes through the drive-thru for something quick and comfy.

She excuses this by claiming that she should not have to cook if she is exhausted and that she deserves the treat to take the edge off the day.

However, after a few weeks of following this routine, she has gained weight and feels unwell. These events contribute to her overthinking and increase her tension. Reaching for delicious eating pleasures has become the source of her stress.

Instead of repeating this harmful cycle, the person pledges to do an evaluation activity every time she would typically give in to the unhealthy need. This person pledges to utilize the time it would take to travel to McDonald's and back, as well as the time it would take to complete dining, to better understand her impulses and cognitive processes. She recognizes that her bad behaviors are the product of bad thinking.

To do this, she will sit and write in a notebook, answering a series of pre-made questions aimed to help her better understand and reject her desire to consume junk food. After this period, the person hopes to have overcome the urge and even replaced it with a desire for a healthy home-cooked, well-balanced meal.

As a reward, this person has provided an additional incentive. If she can maintain her healthy home-cooked meals, she will reward herself with an upgrade in her new quarters. Maybe it's new drapes, new furniture, or new appliances; she has a long list of items she wants in her new house. She determines that if she eats out just once a month, she would treat herself to the newest update she has been eyeing. Six months later, this person has adopted quick, fast, and tasty eating habits, and her new area looks better than ever.

Individuals noticed that their present practices were no longer serving them well. They individually used attention and objection analysis to their present thinking patterns, as well as other mental exercises to cope with internal confusion and tension. They all replaced bad behaviors with good ones, while the approach and intervals of repetition and reward (or punishment) varied.

CHAPTER 8:

COPING WITH WORRYING

Worry is the interest you pay upfront for a loan you may never use.

Do you have to cope with worry and anxiety all the time?

Here are some helpful hints for relieving anxiety and calming your disturbing thoughts.

What is the limit?

Worries, worry, and concerns are quite natural in everyday life. It is our response to it that has the most impact on our life. It's reasonable to be anxious about a first date, a forthcoming interview, or an overdue payment. When worry becomes unmanageable and persistent, it may become overpowering. If you get worked up every day by picturing all of the worst things that may happen to you, you are allowing anxious thoughts to interfere with your life and well-being.

Detrimental thinking, persistent worrying, and anticipating bad results will all hurt your physical and emotional well-being. It progressively weakens you emotionally, draining your energy and leaving you restless and worried, with headaches, sleeplessness, muscular tension, and stomach issues.

The impact on your personal life, as well as your attention at school and work, cannot be overstated. Some individuals find it easier to vent their frustrations on their loved ones and those closest to them, while others turn to drink or drugs or attempt to divert themselves by shutting out everything.

Chronic anxiety and concern are symptoms of Generalized Anxiety Illness (GAD), a disorder that produces agitation, uneasiness, and tension, as well as a sense of discomfort that may take over your life.

If you are plagued by anxiety and worry, you may take a few actions to divert your attention away from them. Worrying repeatedly becomes an issue over time. When repeated, it develops into a mental habit that is difficult to quit. Train your brain to remain peaceful and think only good ideas, and your attitude on life will shift to a more relaxed and confident one.

Why is it so difficult to stop worrying?

Worrying continually has a bad impact on your life. It keeps you awake at night and makes you tense throughout the day. You may dislike the sensation of being worried and confused, yet it is quite tough to stop worrying. Worrying beliefs, whether good or negative, feed this anxiety and may trigger extra worried thoughts in chronic worriers.

Worrying Beliefs That Aren't True

Most people feel that worrying all the time is bad for your health and might drive you insane. You may be concerned about losing control of your thoughts and problems, thinking that they will devour you and eat you forever. Negative attitudes about worrying might exacerbate your anxiety, but good thoughts about worrying can be just as damaging.

Worrying Beliefs That Aren't Negative

You may think, consciously or subconsciously, that you can avoid unpleasant things from occurring to you, plan for the worst-case scenario, and promote remedies. You probably keep fooling yourself that if you worry about something for a long period, you'll ultimately figure it out.

It's much more difficult to stop the habit if you're persuaded that worrying is the most appropriate thing to do in such a scenario and the only way to prevent missing anything. You will be able to regain control of your thoughts once you realize that worrying is not the answer but the issue itself.

How to Get Rid of Worrying

Tip 1: Pick a short period each day to worry.

It might be tough to be productive when your mind is dominated by worry and anxiety, diverting your concentration away from school, job, or family. In this scenario, the method of postponing concern might be beneficial. Instead of suppressing these ideas, permit yourself to experience them later in the day.

Every day, set aside some time for concern. Make a time and location to think about the things that annoy you. Every day, it should be at the same time (for example, 6 p.m. to 6:15 p.m. in the bedroom). Choosing a timetable that will not interfere with your bedtime or contribute to your anxiousness. You might be concerned about anything at this time. The remainder of the day should be worry-free.

Put your concerns in writing. When you have nervous or concerned thoughts, just write them down short and go about your usual activities. Always tell yourself that you can think about it later; there's no need to get worked up over it right now.

During your regular worry time, take a look at your concern list. If your ideas continue to disturb you, allow yourself to think about them, but just for the duration of your worry time. You'll discover that when you evaluate your fears in this way, it becomes simpler to develop a more balanced approach to worrying. If your troubles no longer seem as essential as they once were, just shorten your worry time and enjoy your day to the utmost.

Tip 2: Confront Anxious Thoughts

If you are a chronic worrier and thinker, your perspective on the world may change somewhat. It alters everything, and you may feel threatened as a result. For example, you may imagine only the worst-case scenario and act on your worried thoughts as if they were real.

As a consequence, you may not feel safe enough to face everyday obstacles front-on; you may fear losing everything at the first indication of adversity. Such views, also known as cognitive distortions, include "all-or-nothing" thinking, having a black-and-white viewpoint, and concluding that "if it isn't flawless, then I'm a total failure," or "I wasn't hired for this job; I'll never get any work again." You may create a broad generalization based on a single unfavorable event and expect it to be true indefinitely. That is not how life works.

You may see only the negative aspects of your day, rather than the positive aspects, leading to ideas such as, "I didn't get the final exam question; I'm dumb, and I can't do anything well." Favorable occurrences may be attributed to pure chance rather than your skill to produce positive results.

You may treat your assumptions as facts. With ideas like "I simply know something horrible will happen" or "I know she secretly dislikes me," you may turn yourself into a mind reader or fortune teller. This generates negative energy. Without faith, your mind may quickly leap to worst-case possibilities, such as "The jet is experiencing turbulence; it will crash." You can mistake your ideas for reality: "I feel so dumb; I'm suddenly the laughingstock."

73

You may develop a list of your dos and don'ts and then beat yourself up if you break any of the rules, thinking things like, "I shouldn't have gone there." Now I appear like a complete moron." You may categorize yourself based on your flaws and faults, thinking things like, "I can't do anything properly; I should be a loner." You may accept blame for matters over which you have no control, thinking, "It's my fault my kid died." I should not have left him at the pool alone."

Confronting These Beliefs

Try it out. During your concern time, challenge these negative ideas by asking yourself the following questions:

What evidence supports or refutes these beliefs?

Is there a different way to look at this? Is there a better and more positive way?

What are the possibilities that my concerns will come true? What are the likelihoods? What are some of the possible outcomes in this situation?

Are these ideas beneficial? What impact do they have on me? Do they benefit or harm me?

What would I tell a buddy who is in a similar situation?

Tip 3: Distinguish between solvable and unsolvable concerns.

When you worry, you have less anxiety, according to studies. The moment you're thinking about the issue in your brain, you're diverted from your emotions for a while and believe you're truly solving a problem; in actuality, worrying and problem-solving are two very distinct things.

Problem-solving entails assessing an issue, devising viable solutions, and putting these strategies into action. Worrying, on the other hand, seldom results in any answers. The more time you spend imagining worst-case situations, the less prepared you will be to deal with them if they occur. That is the unmistakable truth.

Is your concern resolvable?

There are several sorts of concerns; some have answers, while others do not. Solvable concerns can be addressed immediately. For example, if you're worried about your bills, you may contact a friend or family to settle them with the prospect of repaying them later.

This form of concern is also known as constructive worry. Unsolvable concerns, on the other hand, are those anxieties that do not have a corresponding action; for example, thoughts like: What if I acquire leukemia someday? What if my family is in a car accident?

Begin looking for answers when you are in a position where you can take action on the issue that is causing you concern. Make a list of all the methods you believe may alleviate your concern. Don't get caught up in looking for the one ideal solution to the situation.

Instead of worrying over problems that are beyond your control, focus on the things that are within your control and can be altered. Create an action plan when you've decided on the answer to your issue. You will be less concerned if you immediately start to resolve your worry.

When the anxiety, on the other hand, is unsolvable, make peace with yourself by being at rest with the unknown. Many of the anxieties of persons who worry excessively are along these lines. When people attempt to predict the future, they tend to worry to feel more in control and avoid probable difficulties.

However, the harsh reality is that fretting accomplishes nothing; life is sometimes unexpected. So, instead of obsessing about things that haven't happened, why not enjoy your life right now?

Most individuals want inner peace: the assurance that everything is and will be OK. But there are times when we worry, create concerns, and consider the same things over and over again without finding a solution.

The tragedy is that we know intellectually that the next exam is not a life-or-death issue. Our kid is most likely not in the ditch just because he or she does not phone at the agreed-upon hour. Our mild headache is most likely innocuous and not a sign of a brain tumor.

However, as our anxiety levels grow, we begin to think in circles or get concerned about failure, and we lose that realistic perspective. We're like living beneath a "dark cloud." Then we can only speculate on what has occurred or will occur. We only see what is wrong in our lives, families, businesses, and the planet. These are, in reality, only thoughts – yet we lose sight of that.

Do you have any fears that something bad or unexpected would happen? What are the chances that these things will happen? Do you worry about the little risk that something dreadful may happen even when the likelihood of bad things happening is low?

Tune in to your emotions and thoughts and pay attention to them. You may conquer your fears by paying attention to your sensations and thoughts while being in the present moment. Learn from your loved ones how they deal with their uncertainties. Can you use their tactics to get over your fears?

Tip 4: Break the Worry Cycle

Respond to the following questions: What am I concerned about?

What options do you have?

Which solution should I go with?

When and how do I put the answer into action?

Simply putting out your concerns might bring some comfort. If you then jot down other answers, you will view your anxieties from a new perspective. You will acquire an observer mindset and be able to think more clearly about what you can achieve.

Meditate. By redirecting our focus, meditation helps to reduce everyday anxieties. We may put the anxieties of the past and future behind us and concentrate only on the here and now. Similarly, meditation may assist us in seeing and comprehending our negative thinking patterns. All we need to do is locate a comfortable, peaceful area and concentrate on our breathing. Several studies have shown that meditation not only helps to alleviate concerns but it may also lower stress and anxiety.

Experiment with gradual muscular relaxation. Sports and exercise can help people relax and sleep better. They also assist to divert us from our daily troubles while also boosting our self-esteem and well-being. This assurance will make it simpler for us to confront our concerns.

Furthermore, studies say that exercise might help not just our anxiety but also our emotional well-being and vitality. Physical exercise, according to several experts, may greatly lessen depression.

Tip 5: Express your concerns.

One strategy to reduce our anxiety is to discuss our concerns with our closest friends. When we are anxious, friends might assist us to calm down and view things from a new angle. They may assist us in seeing the situation from a different perspective. Then, we may frequently discover a remedy or realize that the situation isn't as awful as we thought. Their empathy might make us feel calmer and more comfortable when they listen without judgment or criticism and pay attention to what we say.

It is critical to have someone listen to us with empathy for us to feel better. In other circumstances, professional assistance is also quite valuable if you are unable to discover a way out on your own.

6th Tip: Practice Mindfulness

Most people associate mindfulness with sitting quietly with their eyes closed and deep breathing in a contemplative state. Meditation, on the other hand, is just one example of awareness. Mindfulness is a discipline that does not remove you from your present surroundings, but rather makes you more aware of your current circumstances; it is the practice of impartial awareness.

Being mindful is the sensation of being in the present moment. You accept things as they are, regardless of whether they are good or bad or how they should be. When you are attentive, you are open to the world as it is, without distraction, dwelling on the past, or anxieties about the future. Being attentive entails approaching the present with a fresh perspective as if you were experiencing it for the first time.

Recognize and notice your concerns. Instead of attempting to overcome your worries, observe your thoughts as if they were strangers, without passing judgment. Maintain your attention at the current time. Avoid becoming lost in your thoughts and instead focus on the sensations and things that come to mind. And, if you find yourself becoming lost in your thoughts, draw your focus back to your present surroundings.

Repetition is required every day. To feel comfortable with oneself, make it a habit to practice mindfulness regularly.

How to Engage in Basic Mindfulness Practice Meditation

Make an appropriate location.

It is preferable if you have a separate place set out for mediation. When you reach that place after a while, your mind turns to relaxation mode. An ideal meditation location should be tastefully equipped. If you don't want to commit to a permanent spot, using a particular mat or cushion every time you meditate can suffice. Meditating in a certain location may frequently be quite beneficial.

Put on something comfy.

Nothing is more inconvenient than a pinching waistline or a too-tight collar while meditating. Such little irritants distract from the relaxing impact of meditation and are uncomfortable.

As a result, wear clothes that are both comfortable and do not bind you. It should also match the temperature so that you do not feel chilly even if you remain still for an extended period.

Remove any distractions.

You should not be interrupted while exercising. As a result, inform your family members that you would like to be left alone for the time being, or schedule a period when you will be alone in the home. Turn off your phone or place it in another room where you won't be able to hear it.

Ideally, you should also deactivate the doorbell. Then you may begin your meditation practice without interruption.

Select a meditation pose.

The most common meditation posture is a cross-legged stance. It doesn't have to be that way; you may sit on a chair or kneel on the floor with a meditation cushion instead.

Meditation is feasible even when laying down, although there is a danger of falling asleep soon, which is, of course, not the objective of meditation. Make sure your back is as straight and erect as possible whether sitting or kneeling.

Begin with brief meditation sessions.

Hours of meditation are difficult to achieve at first and are frequently unpleasant for beginner meditators. Such a lengthy period is unneeded. To begin, units of five or ten minutes are sufficient.

Turn off your mind.

Almost all meditations aim to relax your mind. What seems to be easy might be quite tough. You'll probably find yourself being sidetracked by your ideas at first. This is very normal. You must not grow enraged;

you will just become more distracted. Return to your practice after kindly putting the notion aside. It will gradually get simpler for you.

Regular practice is essential.

Meditation, like many other activities, needs daily exercise. The more you meditate, the simpler it will be for you, and you will become more completely relaxed. It is preferable to practice daily, but two to three training sessions a week are also acceptable.

CHAPTER 9:

NEGATIVE THINKING DISORDERS

It's Be Aware, not Beware.

Contrary reasoning disorder is a disorder that stems from severe anxiousness and is sometimes referred to as a tension disorder. Disarrays such as over-the-top urgent problems, summed-up tension issues, post-horrible pressure, alarm issue, and societal worry fall under this kind of turmoil. It is the opposite thinking in these negative reasoning or anxiety issues that feeds the unease and causes it to grow. This point has been established in our deliberations. To remedy it, we need to use techniques such as subjective therapy to transform our negative thoughts into good ones.

It's All the Same and I'm Still Holding On

People who are subjected to the negative consequences of such irrational thinking believe that everything will stay the same and that it will always be bad - nothing changes. By incorporating such a notion into their line of thought, they are closing doors or avenues for assistance. Treatment for such a problem is a standard method, and it involves grasping their perspective.

When it comes to hanging tight, many who have experienced it have had negative or horrifying experiences. They make it more difficult for themselves to break out from the never-ending cycle of animosity and anxiousness by acting in this manner. As they are constantly being thought about, these negative ideas are the essential power wellspring of these scatters. It's one thing to hold on to memory; it's quite another to get fixated on it and become entrapped in a vicious thought cycle. It not only disrupts your daily life, but it also changes your reasoning and may cause you to avoid certain situations and, in reality, confine you.

Absolutes

Those who have a problem with opposite thinking believe in absolutes or boundaries. They see that there must be a bad or good situation.

This may be particularly difficult to handle since they tend to focus on the bad aspects of situations and exaggerate them, overshadowing any favorable aspects. To shift the conventional wisdom, they should realize that stress is normal to some extent and that there will always be advantages and disadvantages, or great and bad in the conditions. They must understand that whatever disadvantage or calamity exists should not be used to control or restrain them. They should figure out what is driving their bouts of anxiousness and fanatical thinking and avoid feeling helpless or powerless. We must all recognize that we are in control.

The problem of opposite thinking may assume numerous shapes and extents, but one component stays the same - the contrary reasoning.

The medicine may assist; nonetheless, towards the end of the day, whatever happens, is something we must deal with in our minds. Early intervention is preferable and is accessible to therapy, ensuring that progress is made as it should be. Life is wonderful; it is not easy, but it is good. Look for it.

Disorder of Habitual Thinking

Defeat It!

It keeps happening over and over again. Your thoughts tend to revolve around relatively same topics again and over. It steadily depletes you. You make an effort to sleep. You can't, though.

There's a buzzing, nagging, annoying voice in your head that won't let you relax. It comes to visit you. You can't finish anything. You understand it has to come to an end. This, old friend, is an illustration of the formal reasoning problem.

I'll never be able to forget it.

Getting rid of impulsive thinking is a difficult task that is proportional to its gravity. Several disturbing thoughts are acceptable and especially normal. Having thoughts that seem to take control of your life; nevertheless, allowing them to leave you mute rather than going forcefully ahead is quite unpleasant. It's plain horrible when you let it draw you back in time and hold you there.

All things being equal, overcoming this problem is not tough. You require it, and you should be excited to concentrate on conquering it since there's a simple solution that might pose to be very difficult if you go about it using the approaches for an enthusiastic reasoning problem. What exactly is going on here?

It is just to focus on good thoughts and have trust in them. Make a reasonable effort to bring oneself into harmony. Once again, everything

84

is more difficult than one could imagine, especially with a good frame of mind formed as a result of this situation.

Goodness Yeah? So, what's the strategy?

The greatest strategy for overcoming mechanical thinking is to try to kill any negative thought that comes your way. When you see that your thoughts are becoming sharper, aim for a good response. You may believe, "I'm not going to have a lot of fun at the gathering," and then say, "but, my pals are there, so it'll be OK." It may be more than fine." It may be difficult to perform at first due to its novelty and polar opposite to what you're used to, but like-for-like

Regardless of your ability, all you need is a little training. Help yourself and don't give up on this one. The more you do it, the easier it becomes and the more it seems to be a programmed reflex.

Beating the critical thinking problem is a chance not only to improve your state of mind or yourself as a person, but it may also improve your life after everything is said and done. Soon, you'll notice that things are looking in your direction and that you're getting to where you need to be in your daily life. Get out of the shadows and view life in a new light.

Thinking, Positive or Negative

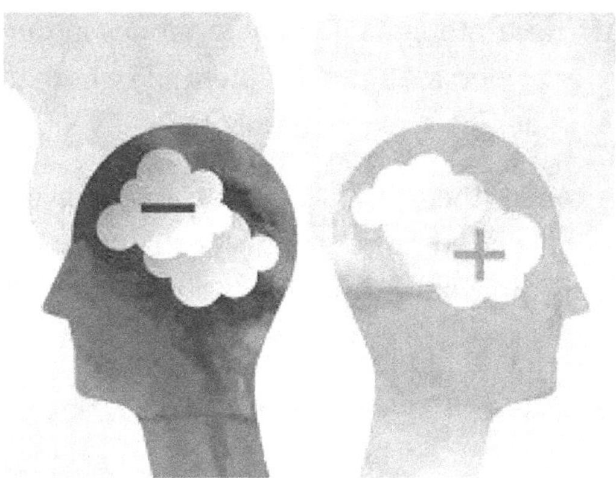

You may now find enough evidence to show that your life is bleak, stressful, and disheartening. You might also gather data to demonstrate that your life is joyful and energetic.

We need to finish an activity!

Examine the space you're in. Is there any residue or dirt visible?

Is there any upheaval? A storage space or drawers that need to be organized? A jumble of documents that should be documented or reused? Is the space in need of painting or repair? Is there a smudge on the light switch plate?

What would your reaction be? Did you find enough evidence that life is horrible, depressing, and overburdening?

Examine the space once again. Do you notice something supplied by a buddy or family that stands out to you? Does it evoke pleasant memories? If you're sitting in a comfortable chair? Do you have a computer on which you may communicate with friends and get acquainted with a broad variety of exciting things? Do you have any flooring that is more aesthetically pleasing than an earth floor? Is there anything there that makes music for you? Is there a CD player or a radio? Isn't it wonderful that we can flick a switch and enjoy the light at any time of day or night?

How would you feel right now? Did you find enough evidence that life is wonderful, clever, and full of wonderful things?

Our thoughts are potent! Those thoughts govern hormones in our bodies, which make us feel better or worse. They also determine whether we have good or bad health, whether we are depressed or joyful.

When people feel disheartened, there is a significant abnormality, but we need to investigate why. God did not create us in this manner. There are a lot of studies out there on what factors affect our well-being.

If you looked about the room and didn't find anything meaningful that didn't come with an unpleasant or negative thought, I'd say you're not thinking clearly. It takes a significant improvement to get your "stinking logic" out the door, but you can accomplish it!

Isn't there anything to be said for positive reasoning? That may be just as bad for you!

Positive thinkers will sometimes use positive thinking to justify their inability to recognize the event.

They have a long list of "shoulds," and unless their circumstances coincide with flawlessness (which happens sometimes), they withdraw into optimistic speculations, assuming they will deliver a better world to everyone with positive articulations.

Some optimistic thinkers have a beautiful sounding way of renouncing.

Concentrating on the positive does not mean ignoring "bad" signs that, if ignored, might lead to burden, worst-case scenario, and disaster, even from a pessimistic position. When we use these bad indications to keep a strategic distance from disaster, they are no longer negative in and of themselves.

Because of disease, we can detect the symptoms of illness and learn all we can to beat that affliction and progress toward that goal. Alternatively, we might begin by stating that "we have" the illness. After claiming it as our own for a long enough period, our mind will generally trust it, and our body may be less tempted to discard it.

We are urged to live in the present. However, a huge fraction of us spend a large amount of the day thinking about the past and also the future, so make it lovely when we do.

Maintain the adjustments! Contrary thinking darkens and horrifies everything. Positive thinking anticipates anything, whether practical or not, whether or not it is related to the event. A few individuals accomplish this by quoting excellent (irrelevant) Scriptures whenever someone mentions a negative incident.

Focus on the bright side! That is not reasoning positively!

There is a time for wallowing in sadness and comprehending current events. It's all about how you handle it. Assuming you won't do anything significant isn't contradictory logic. It is a self-evaluation of one's life and how to make it better for oneself.

To return to the above-mentioned book: "Positive thinking just creates a gap between where you are physically and where you believe you "should" be. A deadly sickness has no "shoulds." You'll be happier and more likely to recover faster if you let go of as many shoulds as you can... It required a lot of contradictory thinking - decades here and there - to speed up the progression of a disease. For what purpose should it be disposed of after 14 days of optimistic thinking?"

Make a deal with intelligence someplace near the sewage and the mists. Concentrate on the good, but keep it genuine. Your mind and body are aware of the difference. Accepting what you believe and say is necessary for health. Your account will not believe the incredible.

Managing Negative Thoughts

We all have unpleasant thoughts from time to time. This is not unusual. Individuals suffering from particular anxiety disorders may have anxiety attacks as a result of opposing thinking. When these attacks occur, the individual's enjoyment suffers greatly.

The problem with anxiety disorders and contradictory thinking is that one bad thought will often lead to a chain reaction of all the more prevalent negative thoughts. These speculations are typically based on self-analysis and might lead the person to believe that the individual in question is, in some way, not exactly other people.

Contrary thinking can be regulated if a person understands a few systems. Once the person has leveled off, he or she may resume living a normal life.

Care is a tactic that is used as part of the habits where you can control conflicting thinking and so modify your behavior.

This is an old practice that teaches the person to focus on his or her surroundings and emotions without passing judgment on either. There are no predetermined outcomes, whether fortunate or unlucky, good or bad, with this approach. Things are what they are, and that's all there is to them.

The person learns how to avoid contradictory thinking, which also calms the nerves and anticipates bouts of tension.

Rather than focusing on what is bothering you, you concentrate on nonpartisan or positive aspects of the situation.

The purpose of this method is not to allow the occurrence of negative thoughts, which, as we all know, feed into progressively negative considerations. You may restrict or eliminate anxiety symptoms by breaking the loop from the start. It also teaches you how to avoid making hasty decisions for yourself when such a decision isn't warranted.

You may also benefit from using confirmations. These are some explanations that you repeat to yourself many times during the day.

These positive explanations are especially useful when negative thought examples are present. Your certificates may be modified to meet any demand, at any time.

Both of these tactics allow you to regain control over your way of thinking. You don't have to put up with opposing arguments if you don't want to. The trick is to replace negative thoughts with happy thoughts.

Whenever you find yourself speculating bad thoughts, fight back with good thoughts or attestations. These repeated good ideas or remarks can assist you to modify your perspective on the situation you are in. You may also maintain a journal of your thoughts and note down which attestations worked best for a certain topic.

Both of these tactics need practice and will take some time to master. In any event, they deserve to be speculated about because they are so remarkable and captivating. They may assist you to live a more pleasant life.

There is a lot of data on each of these systems, whether they are linked to the internet or not. It's your life; take charge of it right now.

Coping with Anxiety Disorders: Step-by-Step Instructions -

Using the Power of the Mind

What goes on in your head influences how you see and identify with yourself and your environment. Finally, at the end of the day:

What you think is what you feel and act upon. A great deal of study has shown that if you are invaded by contradictory thinking, this may manifest as poor confidence, anxiety problems, and wretchedness. Contrary thinking has such a strong causal influence that anxiety illnesses have been labeled as mistakes in learning' by individual scientists.

Furthermore, the link between contradictory thinking and anxiety disorders may take a long time to develop. Many people, for example, suffer from anxiety problems as a result of childhood mistreatment. Such abuse eroded their self-esteem, robbed them of their certainties, and instilled in them the need to question everything and everyone.

Anxiety disorder patients struggle with a wide range of unpleasant or distorted thoughts. The first important step in adapting to anxiety disorders is to study your thinking and seek to detect your unfavorable thoughts.

The following are a few examples of negative thoughts that people suffering from anxiety disorders may experience.

The fear of being objected to People who have an extreme fear of being hated by others become too sensitive to analysis. Their happiness is based on the major findings of others. They are adamant about keeping people optimistic. They may believe that it is difficult to refuse the desires of others. Their demands were discovered to be secondary to the urge to gain the endorsement.

Mental sifting occurs when a person tends to harp and fixate on little negative aspects of even the finest of circumstances, and then uses this pessimism to cast unfavorable judgment on oneself. For example, during a potential employee meeting, one may emphasize that he failed to fulfill expectations since he did not respond to one of the queries that he found acceptable. This might be because the question was minor in comparison to the nine others that he handled well. As a consequence of just one inquiry, the person may begin to perceive himself as a washout.

Mind reading is a situation in which you make assumptions about what other people are thinking based on no evidence. For example, you may conclude that someone dislikes you or believes he is superior to you. Mind readers may have interpersonal problems because they are very suspicious and skeptical of others.

Over-speculation: In this case, a single blunder or error is seen as an example of blunders or mistakes. For example, after crashing his car, the negative person may conclude that he never accomplishes anything correctly and is a bad driver.

The fundamental idea of differentiating negative thoughts that impact you as an anxiety disorder patient is so that you can fight and be free of them. Intellectual Behavioural Therapy provides well-organized guidance on how to combat contradictory thinking and eliminate anxiety problems. On my website, you can find links to online traditional therapy providers on almost every page. Humane cognitive therapy is used in the great majority of these therapies. Anxiety problems may be treated more effectively with cognitive behavior therapy than with medicines.

CHAPTER 10:

MINDSET MANAGEMENT: GOAL-SETTING AND GOAL-ACHIEVING

Obtaining Objectives

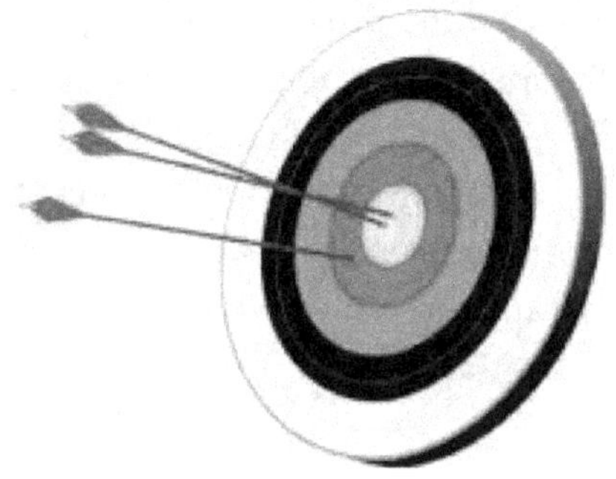

Goal setting is a process that allows you to think about and prepare for your future, as well as drives you to make your vision of how you want your life to be a reality.

Setting objectives is critical for mind reset. You'll become confused, upset, and eventually quit unless you have a defined set of objectives to assist keep your thoughts on track. The nice thing about setting goals is that once you reach them and see firsthand how effective rewiring methods are, it will be the only incentive you need to set additional objectives and work hard to attain them. The key is to cultivate the mentality of good goal planning.

Having a defined approach to goal planning will also allow you to quantify your performance and take joy in moving one step closer to your desired future. This will boost your self-esteem and feeling of purpose tremendously.

Goals do not always have to include altering bad behaviors (but in certain situations, reaching a goal may require changing a bad habit).

Where do you begin?

Everyone has objectives, but they are often hazy. "I want to be a billionaire," "I want to be highly successful in my work," and "I want to be famous" are all reasonable and worthwhile objectives, but until we can be more specific, they will stay more like distant fantasies. They become objectives after you break them down into clear, attainable actions and put a strategy in place to achieve them.

Here's how you do it:

1. Examine your long-term objectives: To begin, consider the large picture of your life in, say, 10 or 15 years. These are your long-term objectives, the pinnacle of your future. "In 10 years, I want to be operating my firm," or "In 15 years, I want to establish a network of profitable dentistry offices," or "In 15 years, I will be rich and living in my dream house."

Finances, jobs, personal accomplishments, relationships, and health are common aspirations. Choose the area that is most important to you as a long-term goal. Once you've mastered the method, you may progressively add more sections.

2. Next, consider what you need to do to achieve your long-term objectives, such as receiving a degree, gaining job experience, or learning about smart investments. These goals are further subdivided into smaller goals that you can accomplish in the next year or six months, then in the next two to three-ninths of a year, and so on until you reach the things you can do right now to get closer to your life goal. 3. Set small specific goals: Make a list of three or four small goals that you can begin working on right away. Always put out your objectives clearly and positively:

4. "I'm going to prepare for and pass my end-of-year test next month." "I'm going to read this book on how to be a successful entrepreneur," or "I'm going to take this ten-day graphic design course," or "I'm going to start my weight loss process by cutting out dessert and replacing it with fruit for the next week." Writing out your objectives can make them seem more concrete and attainable, which will encourage you even more. Begin with one goal and progress to the next when you have completed it.

5. The concept of SMART goals. A SMART objective must have the following characteristics: a. S = Specific, b. M = Measurable, and c. A = Attainable.

d. R= Rewarding and Relevant e. T= Time-bound

Let's apply this to your goal of attending the gym twice a week as part of your larger weight loss goal of losing 5 lbs. in 30 days and your larger weight loss goal of losing 20 lbs. over the following 6 months, and reaching your lifetime goal of becoming and staying healthy and fit.

It's particular. You will set aside two days every week to go to the gym and work out.

It's quantifiable because you'll be able to feel and see how far you've come after a particular time. You will begin to lose weight, your muscles will tone, the fat on your belly will go, and you will feel more energized.

It's achievable because if you continue to attend the gym twice a week, you'll start to see improvements that will lead to you reaching your goal.

It is relevant and rewarding because you want to be healthier, and this goal will assist you in doing so.

It is time-bound since you will have met your objective of losing 5 pounds after a month.

As you can see, SMART goals are indeed smart. Goals are reachable because they are realistic and practical, and the effects can be readily measured. SMART goals have a deadline after which you will begin a new goal or renew an existing one. "In 10 days, I will train my mind to be calmer and less anxious so that I can make this crucial presentation with ease and confidence," for example.

6. Commit:

This entails repeatedly rehearsing the tactics you want to use.

Set aside time for needed practice or activity and stick to it. Ideally, you should have a daily routine, even if it's as simple as 15 minutes of meditation or mindfulness exercises to retrain your mind, or half an hour of reading, practicing skills, or whatever your goal necessitates.

How to Stay Focused

1. Visualize your objectives. Assume your goal is to give a sales presentation to a key client in 10 days. Winning this client's business would be a significant accomplishment for your company and a significant boost to your career. Now imagine yourself delivering the presentation. You're speaking with ease, confidence, and enthusiasm.

The customer and his crew are nodding and listening closely. You can tell they are impressed and enthralled. You finish your presentation and respond to any questions articulately and knowledgeably.

You've sold the client, and you've scheduled a meeting to go over the details. Can you see what you're accomplishing by envisioning your objective in this manner time and over? You are teaching your mind to think optimistically about the future without worry, anxiety, or fear, and this optimism will be mirrored in your actions.

Create a vision board: Making a vision board is one of the most effective and enjoyable ways to visualize goals.

Originally, it was intended to create your goals via the Law of Attraction, but that's a whole other matter! It may be utilized as an effective tool to teach your mind to imagine objectives and make them more concrete for our purposes. Looking at your vision board regularly will convey a clear and consistent message to your brain that these objectives are important to you and make you happy and hopeful.

A tiny bulletin board or a piece of colorful cardboard may be used to create your vision board. Look through publications for images that represent your purpose, resonate with you, and encourage you.

For example, if your objective is to lose weight, seek images of attractive, fit, and happy individuals who you want to appear like after you lose weight. Choose images of happy couples in romantic situations or families having fun together if you want to improve your connection with your partner or become a better parent.

If your objective is to have a larger, finer house, gather images of homes you like, as well as furnishings you'd want to have in your home one day, and so on.

Hang the vision board on your bedroom wall, fridge, or somewhere else you'll see it as often as possible. Spend a few minutes each day looking at it and visualizing your goals to keep them fresh in your mind and motivate yourself.

Excellent advice: I created my vision board in a slightly different way. I gathered photos from the internet and used Windows Moviemaker to make a slide show with soothing music. It was free, and anytime I want to envision my objectives, I just sit down at my computer and start the slide presentation. It's a very calm and pleasurable experience that truly lifts my spirits. Just make sure the gaps between slides are long enough for you to taste and enjoy them. I enjoy looking at my slide show vision board and looking forward to the times I set aside to visualize my goals.

3. Engage in guided meditation. There are dozens of guided meditations on YouTube about goal-setting. Choose from the results for "Guided meditation for visualizing goals." This is a fantastic way to unwind while still focusing on your objective.

Make an "if-then" strategy.

Let's face it: there will be moments when you will confront challenges because life just gets in the way. Dr. Peter Gollwitzer, a psychology professor at New York University, conducted some extraordinary studies in the 1990s. This intriguing research focused on overcoming hurdles by devising an "if-then" backup plan.

He discovered that participants in the study were more likely to achieve their goals when they planned ahead of time and had a plan for what to do if things went wrong. For example, "if I fail the examination, I will get tutoring, study more diligently, and pass the next time." Alternatively, suppose your goal of losing 5 pounds includes foregoing dessert in favor of a piece of fruit. But the holidays are approaching, and you know you'll be tempted to indulge in delicious Christmas cake and cookies. In this situation, your strategy would be, "If I am tempted to eat dessert, I will exercise an additional day a week for one week."

In the worst-case situation, if you fail to achieve a goal, your strategy may be, "If I fail this time, I will learn from my errors, chalk it up to experience, and start anew."

What is the significance of an if-then plan?

First and foremost, it prevents us from telling ourselves negative and crippling self-talk when something goes wrong: "I'm hopeless! I never keep to a routine. I'm a shambles. I'm a loser... I'm done!"

It teaches the brain to make a connection between a hypothetical circumstance, "if," and behavior or response to that event, "then." It protects you from feelings of failure because it gives you a choice.

This plan is referred to as "implementation intentions" in psychology. The subconscious intention and behavior regulation that such plans create in the brain is what makes them so effective for goal achievement.

An effective if-then plan should include the following elements:

A specific response to how you intend to deal with obstacles to achieving a specific goal.

Determine the potential sources of problems. For example, if your goal is to save $1000 in 5 months but you have a weakness for expensive shoes, avoid shoe stores until you have met your goal.

Learn from your mistakes and use them to improve your strategy. For instance, specific scenarios that you should avoid in the future or unanticipated triggers.

Don't beat yourself up when setbacks occur, as they will. Maintain a good attitude and remind yourself that failing is a natural part of life.

Some more pointers for good goal setting

When putting out your objectives, use optimistic language. "I'll save $100 this month by not dining out and instead of having great home-cooked meals." This is a lovely affirmation. What you should not say is, "I will not be dumb and spend money dining out," or "I will accomplish my objective without making stupid errors."

Be as explicit as possible, and specify exact dates if feasible.

Priorities should be established. If you have many objectives, it is usually ideal to prioritize them and focus on one at a time.

Give yourself a treat! When you accomplish a goal, build extra optimism in your thoughts by savoring your victory and giving yourself a hearty pat on the back. Allow your mind to process the accomplishment and how much happiness and delight it brings you. After then, it's time to move on to your next objective!

CHAPTER 11:

IDENTIFYING CORE VALUES

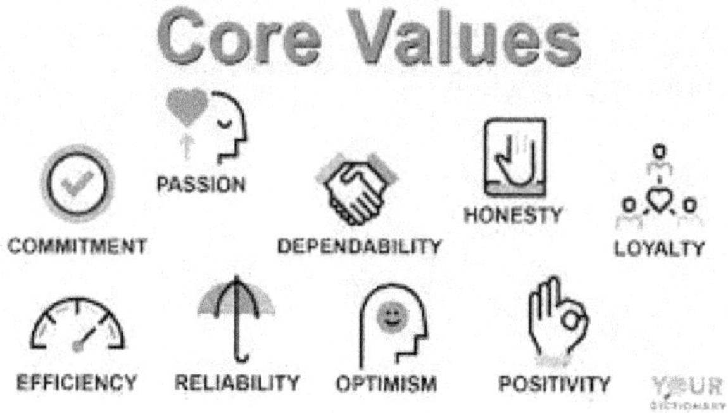

What Exactly Are Core Values?

Core values are beliefs, practices, rituals, and etiquette that you were taught to adhere to. They are the beliefs and traditions instilled in you by your family, friends, and leaders as you grew up. They are beliefs, also known as personal values, that you normally share with others in your social group.

Core values influence how individuals live their lives, connect with others, and make decisions. Core values are not strategies or methods of operation. They do not fall within the purview of competencies or cultural norms. They are not affected by the market, administrative, or political changes, and they are not utilized individually.

Personal connections, educating people, doing business, and making decisions are all guided by our core beliefs. They define who we are and what we stand for. They may assist explain why we do business the way we do and serve as a platform for our companies.

These often vary from one culture to the next, from one family to the next, and from one individual to the next. You will be given a guide, but you are encouraged to improve and adapt the example to reflect your fundamental principles.

To guide personnel, many firms and government organizations create core value statements and mission statements. They are intended to establish a strong feeling of purpose and standards that they try to meet.

For example, the fundamental values of the United States Air Force are integrity first, service before self, and excellence in everything we do. When you read this, you will have a clear understanding of what is expected of you in your employment with the United States Air Force. It is a pledge that every Airman makes when he enters the service.

Let's take a look at some of these slices' sub-categories.

- Workplace Physical Environment Consider the environment in which you work; is it uplifting? Is your environment noisy or quiet, messy or orderly, dull or bright, energy-draining or uplifting? Is there anything alive around you (fish tank, plants, terrariums)? Do you feel comfortable or exposed?

With cubicles and beige paint as they are, there may not be much you can manage at work. But, is your personal space clutter-free and orderly, with a few objects that (if permitted) assist generate a happy atmosphere to help you get the most out of your workday?

Now, I understand that being a K-3 teacher entails some commotion, loud sounds, and exhausting energy. Is it, however, controlled pandemonium and cheerful people singing at the top of their lungs?

On a scale of 1 to 10, how pleased are you with your work environment?

- At-home Physical Environment If you rent, have roommates or have family members whose tastes vary from yours, you may be restricted in what you can accomplish. Consider your home's work and play areas, both inside and out. Do you think they're cute? If not, what do you want to change? Consider your ideal living situation.

On a scale of 1 to 10, how pleased are you with your living situation?

- Career. Is your career progressing at the rate you anticipated or desired? Are you satisfied with your projects, clientele, coworkers, and the company's reputation?

On a scale of 1 to 10, how pleased are you with your career?

- Diet and health. Is your health in excellent shape? Do you have additional weight or stress? How are your blood pressure and sugar levels? Do you use tobacco? Do you consume alcoholic beverages?

On a scale of 1 to 10, how pleased are you with your health and diet?

- Family and friends, Is there anything you'd want to alter about your family relationship? Is there too much planned time but not enough quality time? Is it empty nest syndrome?
    Are you worried about someone else's situation? Is there a lack of participation in family gatherings? Nightmares around the holidays?

On a scale of 1 to 10, how pleased are you with the relationships of your family and friends?

- Spirituality and religion Do you devote enough time to nurturing your inner spirit? This might be in the form of services, volunteer work, or more time spent in nature.

On a scale of 1 to 10, how pleased are you with your religious and spiritual experiences?

- It's personal time. Do you get to take naps now and then?

Spend time with your buddies, maybe without your spouse or family?

There should be some time throughout the week when you are not obligated to work or others.

On a scale of 1 to 10, how pleased are you with your time?

- Income. Are you content with the amount of money you have? Are you able to put aside a certain amount of your earnings? You may not be where you want to be financially, but are you on track with a strategy to get there?

On a scale of 1 to 10, how pleased are you with your financial objectives and savings?

- Recreation and physical activity. Most individuals don't have a lot of time for entertainment or exercise, so we forgo it. This is not a slice to save for later. "The more you do, the more you want to do," as the adage goes.

On a scale of 1 to 10, how pleased are you with your time for exercise and recreation?

Let's have a look at some possible responses. For this example, I'm going to use a 37-year-old mother of two who has been divorced for eight months. She works and has joint custody of her children with her ex-husband:

- Physical Environment - Work (7) - There isn't much we can do about it, but it's a calm work environment with functional equipment and up-to-date software.
- Physical Environment - Home (5) - I never seem to be able to keep up with things. I'm doing okay with getting the laundry done and folded, as well as meals cleaned up. The major rooms are cleaned regularly, however, the other rooms are only vacuumed once or twice a month. And, since the divorce, I've had little time for yard

- maintenance. I can't bear the thought of painting or changing anything while the kids are still in elementary school.
- (8) - I'm fortunate to be able to work in my sector of interest, and it's a terrific firm for working moms.
- Health & Diet - (5) - The doctor thinks I'm 40 pounds overweight. I believe I eat well, but I consume much too much.
- Friends & Family - Friends (8) - I have several circles of friends, including parents from the children's school/events, college students, and coworkers. However, my time has been restricted since the divorce, and I don't see them very frequently. Perhaps it used to be an eight.
- Friends & Family - Family (6) - A large portion of our family still lives in this region, and when I first began dating seriously and graduated from college, I had to establish some limits for my own free time. Maybe that number should be greater; since the divorce, I've seen more of both sides.
- Religion and Spirituality - (8) - both. I keep the kids close to nature, and their father and his family practice the same faith as they do.
- (2) - The only time I have to myself is when I'm getting ready for bed, sleeping, and waking up in the morning.

- Income - (8) - Things are a little tighter now that we have two households, but we're OK.
- Recreation & Exercise - (5) - Once again, time is limited due to all of the children's activities. I don't have much time for fitness, and they are some of the people I've missed. Given all of the changes, I haven't even considered taking a vacation.

Change the chart to fit your life as you have time and think about your responses. Fill out this activity and save it in your work folder. This will be used later in the process of developing your action plan.

As previously said, everyone is concerned. However, you may have observed that some individuals deal with their anxieties better than others. We've all seen an individual who seems to be preoccupied with the issues of everyone they encounter. Then some people never appear to be concerned, and never display that feeling. There are several sorts of concerns.

- Time-sensitive disaster: If an event does not occur within the time frame stated, he or she becomes concerned. The longer the wait, the more time and energy this individual devotes to worrying. Their concerns are exaggerated and focus on the worst-case scenario. Life might feel insurmountable to this worrier.

One of them was my granny. If your aircraft was planned to arrive at 5:30 and you were meant to be home by 6:30, she became concerned if you were not in the house by 6:31. It was stressful for everyone when she asked us to contact the hospital at 7:00 a.m. to check for accident victims.

- **Victim**: This individual has no control over anything. They have no authority, and no one knows what they are doing. They lack confidence in others and believe they have been taken advantage of, tricked, or exploited.
- A worrier with poor self-esteem is a people-pleaser who worries about not being good enough. There is a lack of trust, and this individual wants reassurance from others.
- **Obsessive**: This individual is concerned about their job and production while adhering to strict deadlines. They are highly dedicated to their profession and have very high expectations of themselves and others.
- **Obsessive**: This individual is triggered by everything that goes wrong or does not go as planned for someone in their immediate surroundings. This sort of worrier spends much too much time and energy worrying about matters over which he or she has no control. For this individual, it is a full-time job. They scrutinize every scenario and mentally replay every consequence. You know this type; whether anything occurs on the news, at work, or even to a celebrity, they obsess about it all day. It has an impact on their job and their coworkers.

105

- **Controlled**: Yes, something horrible has occurred, but there is nothing they can do about it. Even if they are worried, they go about their business. Fortunately, we all know some of these folks and should follow their lead. They don't let their anxieties dominate them to the point that they can't think about anything else.
- People are drawn to this person's charm and inventiveness because she is histrionic. To keep people interested in their calling cards, they are constantly courting drama. They don't want to be in the shadows.
- Dependent: This worrier is afraid of being abandoned and exhibits dedication and commitment to the point of becoming clingy and needy in relationships. He or she will go to any length to maintain contact with a buddy or lover.
- **Narcissistic**: This individual feels that he or she is deserving of particular attention, craves adulation, and is concerned with maintaining the image of perfection. Status and status are vital to them, and they are always concerned about others discovering flaws in their armor.
- **Social**: This worrier seems worry-free, but is frightened that their risk-taking and enthusiasm may come at a cost. He or she is continually concerned about the potential for danger. Will this be their last time violating the rules and occasionally injuring other people in the pursuit of having a good time?
- **Passive-Aggressive**: This person is concerned about all the things that may go wrong, or that he or she is not good enough, or is concerned about how much it will most likely cost, rather than focusing on getting the task done. Usually, anticipation is worse than actuality.

They may be concerned about confrontation and stating their truth in front of others. They defy their own and others' desires by procrastinating, being obstinate, or pretending to forget.

Make a note of the sort of worrier you are at the beginning of a new page. List what you worry about throughout the day under your concern type.

Worrier Type: Worrier, Passive-Aggressive	Over-thinking Loop	Efficiency Problem	Sharing Opportunity	Possible Solutions
Unexpected expenses	x			Payment schedule/credit card list
The renter is not making payments.		X		Send information to an eviction lawyer; notify a handyman for cleaning; and penalize the property management organization.
Not suitable for a dance performance	x			Exercise
What are you doing to lose weight for costume	x			Dining

Steps should be practiced three times a day,		x		scheduling - unable to locate notes org
Organize your hobbies/work/ home	x			Schedule and list
Dogs need bathing			x	teach the eldest to bathe little dogs
The kitchen sink is usually clogged with dirty dishes.			x	3 weeks till the conclusion of the meal routine
The house needs a thorough cleaning.	X			Ask for assistance during a family gathering.
Kids do not use the hamper to dispose of their filthy garments.			X	additional routines - family meeting
The wet towel in hamper			X	I'm sick of repeating

				myself at family gatherings.
Create a children's savings account with Ex	X			Make an agenda, just as you would for a business meeting, and adhere to it.
Kitchen Repairs	X			List - Order

Control - Thomas a Kempis, The Imitation of Christ - "Be not furious that you cannot make people as you desire them to be because you cannot make yourself as you wish to be."

Loop Analysis

Do you have the ability to recall certain talks word by word? Why do you believe those specific conversations stayed with you? Let's try we can find out what it was about the subject that irritated you so much.

Make a new page, label it Analysis Loop, and create a left-hand column with the following rows: Who, What, Outcome, Feelings, and Desired Outcome. If you don't have a discussion going right now and can't recall a recent one, go through this material and return to the exercise when you need it.

In the following scenario, the irritated party is a middle manager tasked with implementing new buying software throughout the whole organization. Every firm's department will be obliged to submit supply orders into a single database at Corporate for the corporation to leverage buying power. Corporate owns 21 businesses in the United States.

	Analysis Loop - Why are you going back and forth on this topic?
Who:	Executive Committee (all of your company's department heads)
What:	Before your purchase project, the manufacturing department would want to undertake a project. Problem: Corporate has mandated that all businesses be operational within four months. The production project will need two months of your time, leaving you with just two months to execute.
Outcome:	Production is given the green light for their project (which will need effort from your team to assist with software installation and training).
Feelings:	ineffectual, unsupported, taken for granted, irritability
Desired Outcome:	Greenlight was required to finalize the purchase. project completed before the commencement of the productions project.

Consider how this boss may be feeling. He went into a meeting with the company's top management hoping to gain the go-ahead for the manufacturing project owing to the deadline. Instead, the polar opposite occurs. Some may see this as a vote of confidence in the technology department's ability to complete the task in half the time. However, in this situation, the management thought that the project required the whole four-month time frame.

Now he must work through his disappointment without allowing it to show.

Handle the burden of two projects in half the time allotted for installation. Never mind the day-to-day challenges that every IT department tackles.

Reasons and Importance

The next example is more of an emotional loop. The feeling of Hear Me Now! You want someone to support your vision. Or you truly want to go on an adventure with some buddies or a pal, but it's not going to happen. The fact is that wonderful moment cannot be forced, orchestrated, or recreated. You can't always make people like you or change their minds.

	Analysis Loop - Why are you going back and forth on this topic?
Who:	A running companion

What:	10K fundraising in a new county (rather than the same one you completed last year in your area). You've been supportive of your running buddy's choice of races over the ones you wanted to participate in.
Outcome:	The running companion is uninterested, preferring to do the same races as the previous year.
Feelings:	Frustration, rage, hurt, disappointment, and boredom
Desired Outcome:	A resounding yes 'Sure, let's try something new!'

Sign up for that other race if you're feeling courageous. You may make new acquaintances. You could run across old pals during the event who you hadn't thought to inquire about.

CHAPTER 12:

NEGATIVE PEOPLE AND INFLUENCES

The bulk of our mental clutter is caused by negative conditioning and bad self-talk.

In the long term, harmful negative self-talk may lead to increased stress, decreased immunity, an increased risk of depression or addiction, and a loss in general health. Mastering the skill of regulating negative self-talk is the key to cleaning your mind, overcoming obstacles, gaining confidence, and living the life you've always desired.

Here are some of the most effective tactics for defeating the monster of negative self-talk.

Consider Possibility Thinking.

To make it simpler, consider adopting a more impartial and balanced thinking approach to overcoming negative self-talk. It's difficult to transition to a positive mindset when your mind is being bombarded with more negative self-talk. Consider the many explanations for why something occurred or occurred.

When delivering an unproductive presentation or meeting, consider all of the occasions when your presentation was favorably received by the audience. Make use of cold, hard data. How many meetings have you held thus far? How many of them were fantastic? How many of them were dreadful? What did these meetings and presentations do for you? This results in neutral, balanced thinking.

Just make sure you don't fall victim to the catastrophe or the excessive thinking condition. Possibility thinking is letting oneself realize that, although things aren't perfect, they aren't the end of the world.

One poor presentation does not determine your ability to present or your work ethic. What you're doing is just putting what seems to be terrible things into context (and ensuring that it doesn't happen again).

Try possibility thinking the next time your mind is engaged with highly filtered negative ideas. What are the numerous reasons why something happened? The bulk of the circumstances we encountered was neither blatantly good nor overtly negative, but rather somewhere in the between. To clear your thoughts and get greater achievements, keep your thinking reasonable.

As if it were a loved one, speak.

When you find yourself engaging in nasty mental self-talk, pause and ask yourself whether you'd say anything similar to a close friend or loved one. For example, if your closest buddy fails to ace his or her presentation, would you label him or her as "a foolish person who should never have had the position or is completely unfit for the work?" Why would you tell yourself something so heinous if you wouldn't say it to a loved one? While we find it relatively simple to show compassion and empathy toward others, it's a whole different story when it comes to ourselves.

114

When you criticize or evaluate yourself badly, ask yourself whether you would have said the same thing to a loved one. If not, come to a complete halt. Stop the negative self-talk and consider how you would have responded to a buddy who had disclosed the same to you.

For some inexplicable reason, individuals think it perfectly acceptable to speak to themselves in ways they would never speak to another person. Do you ever refer to someone who doesn't do anything well as a loser? On the contrary, you help them realize that what they are thinking is patently false and that a single failure does not define who or what they are.

Exhibit the same consideration for yourself. We nearly always unconsciously bully ourselves into thinking how horrible we are, causing a slew of mental havoc and destruction. Our expectations of ourselves are often unrealistic and something we would not expect from others. Being harsh on yourself might be beneficial at times, but constantly pushing oneself to be the greatest and creating excessive expectations can be harmful.

Avoid concentrating on previous errors and instead, look forward (as you would usually advise a buddy). Speak to yourself as if you were speaking to a close friend, using a more encouraging and non-critical tone. Replace harsh critical language with more positive terminology. Provide yourself with honest, impartial, and helpful comments. Compliment yourself for the positive things you do, and be supportive about the not-so-great things you do.

To win, spin the wheel.

At times, even changing a few phrases here and there might give your self-talk a more optimistic spin. A little change in semantics may have a significant influence on your subconscious mind, changing your perception dramatically.

On a subconscious level, our ideas and speech patterns are so negative that we don't even recognize we're in negative talk mode. It occurs practically spontaneously and harms the mind. We are so self-deprecating that even when someone praises us, we dismiss it with a "no, that's not true" rather than embracing it gracefully.

Think about how you go to work and support/feed your family every time you are unhappy about having to go to work. You'll notice an increase in happiness and a decrease in stress levels right away. Your thinking will feel cleaner and more rejuvenated.

Avoid Acting like a Victim

Are you one of those persons whose thoughts are always flooded with voices telling you how things are never in your favor or how you have been wronged? Do you often behave as if you have no control over events or as if you are being singled out by everyone?

Avoid playing the victim by blaming outside influences. Accept responsibility for your actions. If it makes sense, you are in control of your life. You have complete power over everything that happens to you.

Even if you can't control anything in your life, you can control how you respond to it. You may either concentrate on the issue and become a victim, or you can find a way to break the cycle. Your response is determined by your decision to be a part of either the issue or the solution. It's futile to continue falling into victim mode. Instead, train your thoughts to take command of your actions and emotions.

For example, the next time you find yourself playing the victim in a bad relationship, ask yourself what caused it. Were your actions to blame for the other person's pain or anger? Did you say or do anything that you shouldn't have said or done? Accept responsibility for your acts without being harsh or too self-critical, and begin working on your flaws to prevent repeating the same errors in the future.

There is nothing you can do to modify your behaviors if you refuse to accept responsibility for them. You keep blaming everything and everyone else, which leads to a self-destructive loop.

Remove the Source

If you want to completely overcome negative self-talk, you must first identify where it originates from. Many times, it is the people around us who shape us to believe or think something is true. Even innocuous or subtle negative remarks or criticism may influence our feeling of self-worth. Others' voices gradually and insidiously become our inner voice of critical self-talk. Never allow someone else's opinion of you to define your reality or serve as the basis for your critical self-talk.

Is there someone around you who sees themselves or your life in a bad light? Are you an unwitting victim of the negativity of others? While negative self-talk is not uncommon, it is often linked back to our training or the beliefs/actions/words of others around us.

Negative critical discourse that stems from another person's lack of confidence or self-esteem is very difficult to cope with. Runaway from such negative and destructive individuals if you want to shift your perspective on life and see things more positively and constructively.

Avoid falling into the negative trap that others have set for you. Avoid chronic, habitual whiners and complainers. Don't legitimize other people's concerns by interjecting yourself or acting as a willing participant.

According to research conducted by the Warsaw School of Social Psychology, persons who are always complaining have worse life satisfaction, more negative emotions, stifled optimistic thinking, and lower moods.

Personalization should be avoided.

You are working on a project with a coworker when he or she requests to be transferred to another project so that they may change their hours to meet the needs of their family. Don't overthink the circumstance and assume he or she doesn't want to cooperate with you.

We all have a natural tendency to personalize things that are not personal. We generally believe that if someone does not pick up the phone or respond to a message because they are presumably driving or at work, it is because they are attempting to avoid us or detest us. Get rid of the habit of blaming yourself for everything that seems to be going wrong in your life. Personalizing and thinking about everything in terms of a disaster are the ultimate spokes on the positive thinking wheel.

Remove Prejudices

Low self-talk is mostly the outcome of a low feeling of self-worth or self-esteem, which stems from self-prejudices.

What we think to be true is often the result of distortion and bias. Get a clear picture of your achievements, talents, and skills. What would they look like to someone else? Do you assess yourself using the same criteria that you use to criticize others?

We evaluate our experiences unconsciously, with a nagging inner voice assessing and judging us on how we've performed in different scenarios. This generates a slew of preconceptions that influence our future thoughts and behaviors (think the mental junk we're dealing with). Replace a prejudiced or biased self-voice with a more objective and rational self-voice. Don't evaluate yourself based on previous events or deeds. Allow yourself a fair opportunity to work with the less-than-ideal items.

118

Accept Imperfections

This is not mean that if you work on a weakness, you should become lazy and accept it. Accepting what you can't alter in yourself and feeling liberated as a result is what accepting your flaws entails.

Make no unreasonable expectations for yourself. While you may strive for a healthy and fit figure, you won't appear like the flawlessly toned model on the cover of a glossy magazine. Keep your expectations of yourself from rising. Some individuals have unreasonable and overly high expectations of themselves and are disappointed, which leads to negative self-talk (and mental clutter). Be kind and fair to yourself. You just cannot do it perfectly every time. You're doing OK as long as you're making progress (however minor it may seem to you). It's okay if you make mistakes from time to time. Rather than being bogged down by previous errors, learn from them and move on.

Your flaws and flaws combine to make you the one-of-a-kind individual that you are. Celebrate your individuality by letting go of self-limiting notions about flaws. Everyone is flawed in their way. Only positive minds, on the other hand, climb beyond flaws by accepting them and moving on.

Give a Name to Your Inner Critics and Rants

Give your inner critic the most ridiculous moniker you can come up with. It will be difficult to take a voice known as "the badger" seriously.

Calling your inner critic something silly adds a sense of levity to it. This assists you in breaking the emotional grip that stress or worry has on you. These short disconnecting circuits, over time, break the whole cycle of stress and worry.

Likewise, give your rants a name. Some individuals prefer to refer to their inner rants as stories or tales. As a result, rather than considering the tirades as facts or the truth, we prefer to see them as habits or

119

recurring patterns. It shows us that the "I can never do enough" tales we heard yesterday are still true today, implying that they are habits rather than facts.

CONCLUSION

The next stage is to remind yourself every day that you are on your path to becoming a better, more complete version of yourself. Take a look back at how far you've gone and be proud of yourself! The key to success, like with everything else, is consistency and dedication. Believe in yourself and your capacity to make the necessary adjustments to achieve your objectives. Once you've cleared the clutter from your head, you'll be able to shift from overthinking to focused achievement daily. "Easier said than done," you've probably heard a thousand times. You should be enthusiastic to learn how to accomplish everything you put your mind to. You've been wanting to make a change for quite some time. Taking the necessary actions to reach your objectives is something that many individuals fail to do.

It's at moments like these, after taking a significant stride forward in my life, that I start to think about how far I've come. It might be difficult to see your success when you are in the thick of things and suffering every day at the start, midway, or even towards the finish of your efforts. Nothing beats going up to the top rung and gazing down to see all of those completed stairs in your wake.

Remember when you were at square one, unable to break free from the bonds of overthinking? I'm familiar with it since I've been there. It takes a lot of guts to stand up and say, "I'm ready to make a difference." It saddens me to think that many individuals spend their whole lives overthinking and overanalyzing, losing out on the joys and appreciation that a free mind may achieve. It is all too easy to get into the comfortable routines of mindless eating, checking your phone or tablet every few minutes, and sleeping later and later until your system is completely out of whack.

It might be all too tempting to give in and allow what's easy to take precedence over what's worthwhile to struggle for. You don't have to be a slave to overthinking, and maybe you can use what you've learned to help transform the lives of others around you.

Perhaps you know someone who seems to be battling with overthinking, worrying over daily issues, and tension, just as you were at the start of your trip. Consider reaching out and sharing your knowledge. Nothing beats sharing fresh information with someone who can use it to produce the same good improvements you've experienced it yourself. It might be a coworker, a spouse, or a close friend. Many individuals from many areas of life will benefit from the improvements outlined in this book, so why not share your experience?